"In 2018—a critical time in our country's history—I had the unique opportunity to advance groundbreaking criminal justice reform legislation—the FIRST STEP Act. As Ja'Ron and Chris describe, the impact of this law will be felt for generations."

—Van Jones,
noted political activist and commentator

"Ja'Ron and Chris formed my go-to team on many matters while we served in the White House together. Their common-sense, bipartisan approach to policy-making was an important element of our success."

—Jared Kushner,
former Senior Advisor to President Trump

"I served alongside Chris while he was General Counsel at the U.S. Small Business Administration, and the passion that he and Ja'Ron share is not only clear, but is coupled in this book with a proven action plan that can result in successful policy enactment."

—Linda McMahon,
former CEO of the WWE, former
Administrator of the SBA, and Chair of the
America First Policy Institute

"Standing up for the forgotten amongst us has always been a critical focus of my time in and out of government. As Ja'Ron and Chris demonstrate, initiatives such as the White House Opportunity and Revitalization

Council and opportunity zone development are just two examples of how conservatives can support our underserved communities."

—Dr. Ben Carson,
former Secretary of the U.S. Department
of Housing and Urban Development

"When it comes to systemically helping underserved communities, Ja'Ron and Chris know what needs to be done and how to do it."

—Bob Johnson,
founder of Black Entertainment Television

"Drawing on the lessons of history and transcending the usual partisan divides, Ja'Ron Smith and Chris Pilkerton outline a bold vision for righting persistent inequalities in our nation. Just as the past ripples through time to shape our lives, we can make change now that will positively affect the lives of Americans in every community and generations yet unborn."

—U.S. Senator Cory Booker

UNDER**SERVE**D

HARNESSING THE PRINCIPLES of
LINCOLN'S VISION for RECONSTRUCTION
for TODAY'S FORGOTTEN COMMUNITIES

UNDER**SERVE**D

HARNESSING THE PRINCIPLES of
LINCOLN'S VISION for RECONSTRUCTION
for TODAY'S FORGOTTEN COMMUNITIES

JA'RON SMITH
and
CHRIS PILKERTON

Post Hill
PRESS

A POST HILL PRESS BOOK
ISBN: 979-8-88845-737-5

Underserved:
Harnessing the Principles of Lincoln's Vision for Reconstruction
for Today's Forgotten Communities
© 2023 by Ja'Ron Smith and Chris Pilkerton
All Rights Reserved
First Post Hill Press Hardcover Edition: September 2023

Cover design by Cody Corcoran

Post Hill Press
New York • Nashville
posthillpress.com

Published in the United States of America
1 2 3 4 5 6 7 8 9 10

To the ones that got us here, like Joe, and to the ones that will carry on the story, like Ramzi and Roux.

CONTENTS

FOREWORD

In the summer of 2020, shortly after the death of George Floyd, we released the Contract with Black America (CWBA). The CWBA is designed to address many aspects of society that need urgent attention regarding both current and historic treatment of the Black community. Its wide dissemination garnered lots of attention, much of it from political circles. Surprising to us, we found politicians from both sides of the aisle receptive. Willing to speak truth to power, we engaged with anyone who could help us address the nonpartisan issue of improving the Black condition, especially when it came to economic opportunity and closing the absurd 12–1 wealth gap between Black and White families.

Ja'Ron and Chris had worked on the passage and implementation of the First Step Act and were also part of the White House team putting together an economic plan for Black America. They reached out to us as part of their efforts; unlike others who paid us the usual lip service, this team was willing to discuss and debate the issues in detail and to integrate many of our ideas into their proposals. We obviously didn't agree on everything (anyone who says they do either doesn't think for themselves or is probably lying), but we held their feet to the fire, especially when it came to establishing a concrete commitment of a half a trillion dollars to directly benefit Black-owned businesses. Chris, Ja'Ron, and the rest of the administration didn't ask for anything in return—no campaigning, no commercials, no endorsement. It was about advancing a solution to a problem we all agreed needed to be solved.

Due to the results of that election, that plan was never able to be implemented. But we continued to work on the CWBA, and Ja'Ron and Chris worked with us—even though neither was still in the government. So far, our work has resulted in the National Football League giving over $150 million in contracts to Black-owned companies, and we continue to work with other Fortune 500 companies and other Black-owned small businesses to ensure that more opportunities in the corporate supply chain get filled.

We don't agree with either party all the time. What we do agree with is helping Black America, which has for so long been overlooked and taken for granted. As such, anyone willing to put in the work—and not just talk the talk—has our respect and attention. This book is about failures and successes. It shows a pathway for many communities to rise—even after decades of letdown and disappointment. The people in Washington call working together bipartisanship, but this issue about helping underserved communities is simple humanity.

We hope people read this book because it lays out ideas for us to work together on these issues—even if they disagree with some of it—because at least it starts the conversation. Standing far apart and screaming at each other hasn't resulted in solutions for people who need it most. Only by opening our minds and having good faith spirited discussions and even disagreements can we arrive at a place of action. Politics is always going to be part of the equation—but if we start from a place where we recognize that everyone needs access to opportunities, we can accomplish more than we ever imagined.

—*Ice Cube and Jeffrey Kwatinetz*

PREFACE

Almost one hundred years before the Civil War, founding father Benjamin Franklin, who would later petition Congress to abolish slavery, traveled from the United States to England.[1] While approaching the shoreline, his vessel came under great stress and danger from the rocky shoals and dramatic currents. While Franklin made it safely to ground, he wrote to his wife about this incident during his voyage, stating, "Were I Roman Catholic, perhaps I should on this occasion vow to build a chapel to some saint, but as I am not, if I were to vow at all, it should be to build a light house."[2] It is with this intention that this book has been written. This country has seen, and in many respects continues to see, very turbulent times. And regardless of race or religion, this country needs a path forward that must be walked by our people and our leaders

---

[1] "*In 1789 he wrote and published several essays supporting the abolition of slavery and his last public act was to send to Congress a petition on behalf of the Society asking for the abolition of slavery and an end to the slave trade. The petition, signed on February 3, 1790, asked the first Congress, then meeting in New York City, to 'devise means for removing the Inconsistency from the Character of the American People,' and to 'promote mercy and justice toward this distressed Race*," "Benjamin Franklin's Anti-Slavery Petitions to Congress," The National Archives, https://www.archives.gov/legislative/features/franklin#:~:text=In%201789%20he%20wrote%20and,end%20to%20the%20slave%20trade.

[2] *Benjamin Franklin*, directed by Ken Burns (PBS, 2022).

together. However, that path must be illuminated by the lighthouse of intentionality—a concept that the reader will be very familiar with by the end of this book. This work seeks to add a few bricks to the construction of that lighthouse so that our collective journey will result in safe and sustainable passage.

When Ja'Ron was growing up in Cleveland, Ohio, everything he knew about political history originated from the perspective that conservative Republicans wanted to oppress Black people. He believed it was actually the Democrats—both liberal and progressive—who were the champions of social advancement and were those seeking to address the issues of racism and poverty. However, Ja'Ron was not aware of the nuances of what it meant to be conservative or liberal, and he certainly was not aware of the foundations of either ideology. His introduction to society started in ways that may be familiar to many Black Americans. He clearly recalls the first time he was called a "nigger." It was 1992, and he was eleven years old living with no heat or lights, because his family's bills had gone unpaid. He was a self-described "angry young man," as he had determined that others might view him as something less than who he truly was. This belief was coupled with the fear that he might never get the chance to prove to them that he was anything different. Somehow, however, he knew that this apparent reality would not define him, and more importantly, he sought to make it his life's mission that others in similar circumstances who were unable to advocate for change would not be characterized by those conditions.

But how would such a young man actually do that? Role models like Dr. Martin Luther King Jr. and so many other civil rights leaders preached about nonviolent protest, but at the same time, leaders like Malcolm X advised more active resistance. It was a lot for any Black person to digest—but perhaps especially so for a young Black man in this urban environment. Ja'Ron's father focused on the basic building blocks of education so that Ja'Ron could make decisions about how to establish his own path—which was much more difficult than it seemed. His neighborhood was full of violence, and those that were making their way in the world seemed to be the toughest people on the block. This translated into his initial world view that physical dominance was a critical component of any kind of advancement.

While Ja'Ron didn't engage in the gang activities, he still needed an outlet for what was building up inside him. High school football became that outlet—but also provided him with much-needed discipline and experience in goal setting. As with so many others both inside and outside of underserved communities, sports became a genuine avenue of teaching and training for him, and a perfect way to see hard work translate into success. An injury cut that on-field experience short, but the lessons remained.

Trying to determine how to advance without his physical strength, Ja'Ron turned to his father's instruction and focused on his education. While certainly not a stellar student prior to his football injury, Ja'Ron redoubled his efforts. He went from potentially being expelled from school for both behavioral and academic reasons, to becoming a strong student leader. While the temptations of gangs and criminal activity were always present, he knew that he must not consider that avenue. He knew that his approach to life must include an examination of the underlying reasons for socioeconomic circumstances—and that he must find those out on his own.

Ja'Ron did not really start out as a liberal or a conservative; as mentioned, he didn't even really know that those terms meant. But as he discovered things for himself, he saw that many of the people helping him along his journey—his teachers and coaches, for example—were in fact conservatives. Reading authors like Ralph Waldo Emerson, he established the foundational principles for what his core philosophy would become: a concentration on self-reliance. His critical thinking skills developed, and he taught himself to see through circumstances and to not blindly accept one side's politics over the other. This ability became stronger every day as he continued to see what was happening in his community—as drugs and alcohol addiction perpetuated a vicious cycle of poverty and prison for so many in his neighborhood. As he discovered other authors, like Rudyard Kipling, who espoused being the master of one's fate, he knew that it would be up to him to decide how to approach solutions to the problems he was seeing and dealing with firsthand.

Ja'Ron's struggles speak to the challenges of so many Black Americans, as well as so many others in underserved communities. Hurdles—in the form of a lack of role models, education, training, capital, or what have you—are omnipresent. There are of course significant historic components to these challenges, and many of them have become systemic across many communities. Crime, violence, and the associated traumas are not so easy to shake off. They live with a person and can easily cause their personal downfall.

Chris' experience was different. Growing up in the suburbs of Washington, D.C., he was not exposed to daily violence or crime. His parents provided a very comfortable upbringing, but also stressed the importance of education and the concept of service to others. Chris wound up at his father's alma mater: Gonzaga College High School, a Jesuit institution just blocks from the U.S. Capitol building. For those of you who do not know the Jesuits, it is a group within the Roman Catholic Church technically called the Society of Jesus.[3] Its founder, St. Ignatius Loyola,

---

[3]   It is important to be clear that the while the Jesuits have undoubtedly impacted many individuals in order to advance social justice efforts, the organization did have historical engagement in the slave trade. Adam Rothman, a historian at Georgetown University has stated that *"the idea was that the Jesuit plantations manned by enslaved people would essentially subsidize the Jesuit educational mission."* H. L. Gates, *The Black Church* (Penguin Books, 2021), 55. It should be further noted that Georgetown University has publicly acknowledged this history: *"In 2015, Georgetown University President John DeGioia established the 'Working Group on Slavery, Memory and Reconciliation.' The working group's efforts led to a formal apology from the Jesuits and the creation of the Descendants Truth & Reconciliation Foundation, announced in 2021 as a partnership formed*

established a vision of seeing God in all things and seeking a commitment to service and justice. Loyola was the son of a nobleman, and during his military service, he had a significant injury that left him bedridden, with only biographies of saints to read. This in part led to the founding of the order and its focus on education. The Jesuits have the tongue-in-cheek nickname of "God's Marines," as their approach to ministry and education incorporates global outreach. In fact, Loyola often ended his letters to his fellow Jesuits with "*Ite, inflammate omnia*" ("Go set the world on fire").[4] This phrase reflected his desire for his colleagues to educate in a manner that showed God's passion and zeal for humanity.

Chris found this approach to education very compelling, and it associated all learning with how one could use the knowledge gained to help people. Much like Ja'Ron, education became the tool for Chris that would light the pathway to helping others. This idea became even more entrenched in him as he became engaged in the many social outreach programs at Gonzaga—such as the famed Father McKenna Center on campus, which so many Gonzaga students participated in to feed the homeless of Washington. Chris went on to a Jesuit college, Fairfield University. There he utilized his favorite subject—politics—as an educational foundation to affect change. He was among the first students to run for local town council, and the first to contemporaneously serve as both a town council member and the student body president. He used this combination of roles to address campus issues of race relations as well as to foster student

---

by the Jesuits and the GU272 Descendants Association. The Jesuit order pledged to raise $100 million for the foundation's work, which will support educational opportunities and scholarships from early childhood education to higher education for descendants of the 272 enslaved men, women and children." See Chaz Muth, "Georgetown Officials Say Amends for Slavery Past Are Ongoing and Long Term," Crux, April 16, 2022, https://cruxnow.com/cns/2022/04/georgetown-officials-say-amends-for-slavery-past-are-ongoing-and-long-term.

4   Jim Manney, "Go Set the World on Fire," Ignatian Spirituality, https://www.ignatianspirituality.com/go-set-the-world-on-fire/.

service within the larger community. He would also be fortunate to engage on mission trips to work directly with the poor as part of his experience at Fairfield. Once again, much like Ja'Ron, he knew that a calling was wrapped up somewhere in all of this, and while he does not describe himself as a patient person, he is very aware that things like this all happen in God's time. While not attributable to the Jesuits per se, a meaningful adage in considering these journeys is: "I'm not interested in whether you've stood with the great; I'm interested in whether you've sat with the broken."[5]

Chris recalls one particularly impactful Jesuit professor who taught a first-year religion class at Fairfield, where students studied books across the religious and social spectra. The professor required two things from the students in addition to completing the assignments. First, if they didn't understand a word or a concept during a lecture, they were required to say "stop!" If someone did not stop the professor within five seconds of his uttering an intentionally difficult word or concept, he would require a classwide pop quiz, the result of which would either add or subtract a full point off each student's final grade. For whatever reason—the students' youth, shyness, or embarrassment—a few pop quizzes took place in the wake of no one stopping the professor. But after they dropped a few grade points before even taking a real test, people stopped him pretty frequently, and everyone learned together. Second, while reading a book, whether it was the Bible, the biography of Malcolm X, the speeches of Martin Luther King, or the work of another author, a student would have to ask the professor a question as if they were the author—in other words, forcing the students to put themselves in the place of the individual whose writings they were asking about. These two approaches to learning not only became cornerstones to Chris' approach to critical thinking, but helped to establish that putting oneself in the place of others and truly empathizing with them is crucial to any holistic policy approach.

---

5   Sue Fitzmaurice Quotes, https://www.goodreads.com/author/quotes/4207373. Sue_Fitzmaurice.

Twenty-five years later, after almost three years serving as general counsel and then acting administrator at the U.S. Small Business Administration, in late 2019, Chris was asked to come to the White House to meet with Jared Kushner, then senior advisor to President Donald Trump. The meeting was brief, and Brooke Rollins—the head of the Office of American Innovation and future head of the Domestic Policy Council—was also present. Chris had previously met them both briefly in presidential cabinet meetings, but he had not spent much time with either of them. They welcomed him into Jared's office, they all sat down, and Chris was asked the question that any student of public policy might be a little intimidated to hear just steps from the Oval Office: "What do you want to do next?"

Chris knew instantly that this covered the gamut of the entire federal government, so the next words out of his mouth would be important. Having been a financial crimes prosecutor and securities regulatory attorney for much of his earlier career, he first thought that the Department of Treasury would be a reasonable destination. But then, relying on his Jesuit roots, Chris went to a problem that had been vexing our society for far too long, and one that he had been exposed to early in this journey. So he answered, "homelessness." They discussed a general approach to address the issue of national homelessness, and then Chris left the White House campus—still blown away and filled with a unique sense of patriotism. Shortly thereafter, Brooke called Chris, asking if he would lead the White House's Opportunity Now program. It would be an all-of-government approach to address all issues for underserved communities, including economic development and poverty—certainly a larger portfolio than had been discussed in their first meeting. As will be discussed throughout this book, that role at the White House developed almost contemporaneously with the COVID pandemic. But that meeting and those people would directly impact Chris and his family a short time later.

In June of 2020, after Chris had been working at the White House for just a few months, his older brother took his own life—a casualty of sorts of the pandemic. In the midst of his and his family's grief at the funeral, Chris looked up to see…Jared, Brooke, Ja'Ron, and his White House colleagues Steve Smith and Charlton Boyd, as well as the accompanying security detail. They had surreptitiously gone to the funeral to support their friend and colleague.

That night, after all of the funeral attendees were gone, Chris sat with his young nephew at the kitchen table. The boy asked his Uncle Chris if he had seen the Secret Service members that had been there for his papa's funeral; he took their presence as a sign of respect for his father. And frankly it was—as it was his papa who had imparted so much of his time, energy, and wisdom to Chris, resulting in his working with these folks in the first place. Chris will never be able to express how much their presence meant to him on the darkest day of his life, nor will he be able to adequately convey their contribution to his nephew's perception of that awful time. The very next day at 8 a.m., Chris met with Jared in his office in the West Wing and was given the green light to initiate a draft presidential executive order on mental illness and suicide—tragedies that plagued so many families in 2020 and still do. The executive order, entitled Saving Lives Through Increased Support for Mental and Behavioral Health Needs, was signed by President Trump on October 5, 2020.

So given their different backgrounds and upbringings, are Ja'Ron and Chris an unlikely pair to coauthor this book? Perhaps. But it is their collective experiences that allow them to take on the issues discussed within these pages. It is their singular commitment that not only fuels a vision for our country's underserved communities, but does so in a way that underscores that immediate actions can lead to transformational results. People will not have to hope and wait for opportunity if our society decides to follow a plan that reexamines civil society and rediscovers what it means to be an American.

CHAPTER **ONE**

Defining the Problem

It was February 7, 2020, in Charlotte, North Carolina. A national policy summit initiated by the Trump White House titled Opportunity Now had been scheduled to take place at Central Piedmont Community College. This was supposed to be the first of dozens of meetings that would usher in a new era of public and private partnerships all across America. For the first time in history, all of the key federal and state agencies with resources for underserved communities would provide aligned direct technical assistance to local residents on a number of programs focusing on areas including economic development, entrepreneurship, workforce, and housing. The event featured local, state, and national private and public sector leaders discussing a number of topics, and the goal was to engender a shared strategy for empowering the underserved in Charlotte and throughout North Carolina, which would then become a blueprint for the entire country. This event was only a first step toward moving these communities forward, and it was positioned to set an example to be applied in other states and cities. Then, just a month later, when the organizers were in the midst of preparing the same opportunity for

Miami, the whole world changed as we all fell victim to the coronavirus. The strategy was forced to change, but the mission endured.

The title of this book, *Underserved*, refers to all of the forgotten communities across this country. The goal of helping these communities was meant to be addressed during the Reconstruction phase of history at the close of the Civil War. While this somewhat utopian idea of President Abraham Lincoln's did not have nearly the successes that were envisioned, its legacy—both the good and bad elements of it—remains deeply entrenched in the United States. Over one hundred and fifty years later, politicians continue to give lip service to these socioeconomic realities, but the fact of the matter is that deep disparities continue to exist. The Opportunity Now summit in Charlotte was supposed to be the first example of an intentional strategy to change the trajectory for underserved communities, but between the COVID pandemic and the results of the 2020 election, time simply ran out. And given the strategy's inability to be consistent and intentional, the stark differences in economic opportunity across our country continue.

It is just a fact that these disparities exist—a fact that certainly will not change with campaign speeches and nonspecific never-ending government programs. The simple question that stands before the country is: What is the plan for these disenfranchised communities? And the question for the conservative movement is: How do we address it in a meaningful way that is consistent with conservative principles? The answers to both questions have unquestioned human consequences, as well as significant political realities. Republicans sometimes use certain clichés when referring to their party, such as "the party of Lincoln" or "a big-tent party," but without a specific strategy that outlines how these communities can be materially assisted—one that is consistent with traditional conservative ideology—clichés such as these will be deemed hollow by the national electorate.

To introduce the relationship of the authors a bit more, Chris and Ja'Ron first met while working in the Trump administration. Their paths crossed because of their shared focus on creating solutions to the issues that plague underserved communities—issues like access to capital, lack of jobs and opportunity, economic dynamism, and lack of public safety. At the time, Chris was serving as general counsel at the U.S. Small Business Administration (SBA), and Ja'Ron was serving as the special assistant to the president for legislative affairs and director of White House Urban Affairs. A typical presidential administration establishes something known as a presidential coordinating committee, or a PCC, which does much of the work after the announcement of a presidential executive order. In these meetings, all relevant cabinet agencies are represented—typically by deputy secretaries or other senior policy officials within the agencies, but rarely (if ever) by general counsels.

The PCC on which Chris and Ja'Ron met had been formed as part of the executive order establishing the White House Opportunity Revitalization Council (WHORC), and the day they met, it was being led by Ja'Ron as the director of Urban Affairs. This PCC announcement came across Chris' desk not as an invitation but rather as a simple agency notice. Given his interest in the topic, Chris joined the assigned SBA representative in the Treaty Room of the Old Executive Office Building on the White House campus. There he first heard about Ja'Ron's vision for supporting underserved communities and about the impact that all of the agencies around the table could have to advance this mission. It was not yet a full plan, but rather a promise that would help shape the thinking set forth in this book.

That moment in time has passed, and much of Ja'Ron's original vision was transformed by the impact of the pandemic. But now, without the power of the White House and the command of the specific executive agencies, conservatives must regroup and determine where this issue falls in terms of priority and how they—as members of a party and a community—can determine a dedicated way forward. One critical notion here is that the necessary strategy for underserved communities must be crafted by principled conservatives who have seen the process from the inside of government. Chris and Ja'Ron have worked at the highest levels of a presidential administration—one serving as a cabinet member, one counseling the vice president, and both advising the President of the United States, governors, and mayors on critical issues of economic development all across the country during one of the most consequential times in the history of our republic.

Ja'Ron has worked for some of the most notable politicians in the current conservative movement, including Vice President Mike Pence, Senator Tim Scott, and Representatives Jim Jordan and J.C. Watts. While serving in the White House, he developed groundbreaking legislation that has been deemed critical to underserved communities. This legislation concentrated on topics such as opportunity zones, permanent funding for historically black colleges and universities (HBCUs), and the First Step Act's criminal justice reform—which in part focused on the rehabilitation and reentry of prisoners into our communities—as well as the WHORC, which was publicly launched at the Opportunity Now summit in Charlotte.

During this time, Chris served at the SBA. Even before the implementation of the Paycheck Protection Program (PPP) to support businesses and their workforces during the pandemic, he committed certain agency efforts to outreach and access to capital, workforce development, and technical assistance programs for underserved communities, as well as his spearheading of a first-of-its kind series of conferences to enhance employment opportunities for the disabled, foster youth aging out of the system, and the formerly incarcerated. He had the good fortune of working for Linda McMahon during her tenure as SBA administrator, and his time succeeding her in that role allowed him to continue the many impactful policy initiatives that she had championed, including significant cross collaboration with key agency partners, such as the Departments of Education and Labor.

In March 2020, Chris and Ja'Ron teamed up at the White House. At the time, Ja'Ron was serving as the deputy director of the Office of American Innovation, while Chris had been appointed to run the formal national Opportunity Now program. In that same month, COVID repositioned the priorities of the country, but the team remained committed to how all of these changes would impact forgotten communities and was poised to continue its work however possible. Working directly with Congress, leaders of the National Economic Council (NEC) Larry Kudlow and Andrew Olmem, the Domestic Policy Council (DPC), the Office of Management and Budget (OMB), the Department of Treasury, and other White House and cabinet officials and their agencies, the team developed and debated numerous economic responses to the COVID pandemic—serving as the face of the PPP to many by conducting dozens of informational webinars for groups that represented urban and rural areas—particularly communities of color. Team members spoke to dozens of governors and mayors of both major parties to assess where the federal government programs could be rethought or amended to enhance access to capital and workforce training and job placement opportunities. They engaged with countless local chambers of commerce representing various regions and demographics, as well as with bank executives, foundations, philanthropic icons, and members of Congress, to craft approaches that could redeploy existing federal dollars to enhance opportunities for these communities.

These efforts included meetings with the key members of President Trump's cabinet to ensure that their agencies were maximizing existing program and human capital resources for this effort, as well as performing a top-to-bottom scrubbing of appropriations across the federal government with the OMB and NEC. In fact, this effort even resulted in the submission of draft legislation to key lawmakers that included things like the permanency of the federal government's premier organization to support minority business—the Department of Commerce's Minority Business Development Agency (MBDA)—which came to pass in a bipartisan manner in the next Congress.

Chris and Ja'Ron also cowrote and delivered on presidential executive orders, including on the topics of police reform in the wake of the summer 2020 protests, bringing leadership from national law enforcement and community activism groups together in the same room and hammering out mutually agreeable and meaningful federal actions on police training, precinct accreditation, support for those impacted by mental and behavioral health challenges, and care for the homeless. Of note, this executive order on police reform was replaced in May 2022, but as will be discussed, its replacement was ostensibly a mirror image of the order that had been written two years earlier.

Finally, Chris and Ja'Ron worked together in October 2020 to develop President Trump's Platinum Plan—a one-of-a-kind strategic platform for economic development that sought to use and streamline existing resources and programs to create economic prosperity, social responsibility, and market-based opportunities for Black communities. This policy document incorporated the thoughts and input of Black leaders on both sides of the aisle, well-respected community activists, and other key cultural leaders in the Black community—including famed musician, actor, and icon Ice Cube. Similar plans were developed for other minority communities—all of which were tied to real dollars and actionable items for a second presidential term.

The authors of this book's abilities to adeptly communicate with, coordinate through, and develop trust among public and private sector individuals and nonpartisan coalitions were critical to the behind-the-scenes efforts to support underserved communities during this time. And needless to say, that experience is germane to this conversation, as the road map for systemically addressing these communities in a consistent and market-based way in non-pandemic conditions is critical to the future of our country. Extreme solutions of spending are either socialist in nature or historically so unimpactful that the results are easily predictable with even a passing knowledge of past efforts. A never-ending cycle of money creates dependence. But there is a way to reframe this problem so that the answer becomes clearer, so that it does not become a choice of trillions in spending versus a strict version of insisting folks pick themselves up entirely by their own bootstraps.

The problem society is faced with is truly a market failure for our country—not unlike a massive financial crash or other significant crisis. And when markets fail, chaos can ensue. And to a certain extent, that is what happened over the course of the COVID pandemic—race-based riots, unmitigated violence, and other undesirable social consequences. Just as with other market failures, if something is not done, the destruction and degradation of our society will continue. It might go slowly, but it will more than likely accelerate over time. And if it does, it will cause a market failure of such proportions that any response will simply mitigate the inevitable at best. We must take action now to prevent this while we still can.

Any response to such a crisis is always difficult and uncomfortable to a certain extent, but it often requires a massive change in thinking to overcome the unthinkable. And more importantly, it requires a clear pathway forward that incorporates a committed strategy and thoughtful execution, as well as a meaningful and planned transition from that approach when the foundations of that newly formed strategy are strong and resolute. Many current media and political pundits throw out half-baked thoughts as if they are hucksters and tonic salesmen from the Wild West. Just like the con men and women of old, today's pundits can make a few dollars by going from town to town—or to blogs and cable TV shows—considering "likes" or high ratings to be signs of success as opposed to measurable results and progress. They oftentimes frame a problem in a manner that will profit them most. Their strategy is always to blame someone else, and once that is achieved, they can seek the political profit of an ideological convert by simply highlighting a decades-old problem and offering no solution and no concrete plan to address these ills.

This is where that ends. This book addresses this modern-day market failure in the context of some of the most well-known conservative thinkers in our history. It presents a historical background of certain actions, goals, and visions, coupled with a clear and precise framework for how we can collectively address this market failure, and do so in a way that is consistent with conservative ideology.

But from where does this originate, and what can be learned from the history of these issues? While dramatic social and economic shifts have been proposed and undertaken—and have succeeded or failed—at many points in our nation's history, no greater opportunity for change was missed than during Reconstruction. As will be discussed herein, Reconstruction was chiefly about the end of the Civil War and the plan to preserve the Union. This was a plan that had been envisioned by President Lincoln, was nurtured by Black leaders such as Frederick Douglass, and then was sought to be resuscitated by President Ulysses S. Grant. Lincoln's assassination, President Andrew Johnson's ascendancy, and the associated politics of the day ultimately extinguished the promise of what Lincoln had conceived. The vision was for much more than buildings and railways; it was about the integration and assimilation of the human experience for the people of the United States. Of course, former slaves were a critical part of that, but the plan included poor White Southerners and other disenfranchised people who would be given a foundation and foothold for access and opportunity. It was not a system of quotas or preferences, but rather a plan to foster a fairness that would speak to the essence of American idealism.

This book explores that idea and where it is today. Its analysis is conducted through the dual lenses of the intent of Reconstruction and the state of affairs for American underserved communities of the twenty-first century, by extrapolating the principles of Reconstruction and applying a strategy that conservative ideology can embrace to heal wounds that simply must be healed. Call it morality, call it humanitarianism, call it market failure or a matter of national security, but not only is an open discussion of this type needed; a specific plan must be articulated. This plan must be consistent with the founding principles of this country and with capitalist and competitive economic views, and must begin in a concentrated and committed way. Piecemeal construction does not build a building, and it certainly does not build a community. And now there is a chance to embrace a plan that is thoughtful and holistic.

The book begins with reviewing some of the history around Reconstruction—its intents and what went wrong. It then explores how these failures developed over time and connects the plan to some of the modern era's social and economic challenges for underserved communities—showing these issues as examples of a not-so-traditional slow-moving market failure. As part of this analysis, it examines the guidance of some of history's most identifiable conservative thinkers, as the principles set forth by these thought leaders will be critical to the development and formulation of the ultimate proposal. The work of individuals such as Edmund Burke, Alexander Hamilton, Alexis de Tocqueville, Friedrich Hayek, Milton Friedman, Jack Kemp, and Thomas Sowell will help to direct and shape this plan, and this book will offer specific quotes and anecdotes to demonstrate to the casual reader, academic, think tank executive, civil servant, and elected official that the approaches set forth herein are consistent with conservative principles. The chapters then unfold to demonstrate what empirically has and has not worked to address the problems of underserved communities in the past, and highlight how some of these problems' more foundational elements were addressed during the years of the Trump administration. This will lead us to a discussion of the social determinants of an economically efficient ecosystem, what components are currently in place, and what policies can be adopted to enhance market-based outcomes.

Finally, the authors' approach embraces a deep knowledge of federal and state government functions in order to present readers with a specific action plan that identifies the problem, addresses the problem, approaches these issues with data-driven solutions, and empowers traditional free-market principles of true conservatives, ultimately returning responsibility for the underserved communities to civil society. The term "civil society" is defined as "society considered as a community of citizens linked by common interests and collective activity."[6] Conservative organizations such as the think tank The Heritage Foundation seek to build on this by advocating that families, religious institutions, and individuals are at the heart of America's thriving civil society, providing for the welfare of communities in ways that the government cannot—a concept at the center of the solution discussed within these pages.

Back in his days working in the U.S. Congress, Ja'Ron launched something called the Anti-Poverty Caucus as part of his work with the Republican Study Committee. Partnering with The Heritage Foundation and The Woodson Center, his team concentrated on training these congressional caucus members on how private sector solutions could be developed to address and combat poverty. These solutions were found in the familial and community institutions that were beyond the reach of government bureaucracy or the unenforceable promises of political candidates—places such as community centers and houses of worship. It is these critical institutions that must be at the center of our civil society, because a perpetual social safety net not only establishes a debilitating

---

6   See Hannah Nivar, "A Lost Generation and the Breakdown of (Civil) Society as We Know It," *Northeastern University Political Review*, March 28, 2021, https://www.nupoliticalreview.com/2021/03/28/a-lost-generation-and-the-breakdown-of-civil-society-as-we-know-it/.

dependence but also is a limiting factor that does not allow individuals and their communities to experience their full and collective God-given potential. By reimagining what these pillars can look like, we can reembrace the foundations of civil society and ensure that they are incorporated into a holistic strategy that takes the underserved from a place of mere survival to a place of true prosperity.

The authors invite the reader to engage with an objective lens, and to rely on both their common sense and perhaps uncommon experience to gauge the rationales and the eventual proposal offered. While partisan identity cannot be decoupled from this text, the reader is ultimately the decision-maker in determining whether the current approach has resulted in the best that our country can do for these communities now and for generations to come. The approach posited seeks to embrace our country's military philosophy of leaving no one behind; however, just like in the military, it must be drenched in discipline, commitment, and a recognition that we are all ultimately on the same team. As Lincoln said, "Let us have faith that right makes might, and in that faith, let us, to the end, dare to do our duty as we understand it."[7]

---

[7]   Scott Horton, "Lincoln—Right Makes Might," *Harper's Magazine*, February 12, 2010, https://harpers.org/2010/02/lincoln-right-makes-might/.

CHAPTER **TWO**

Lincoln's Vision for Reconstruction

Intentionality is a rare thing in Washington. This does not refer to someone's belief system, but rather the ability to set a specific path and walk that path regardless of public polling or media commentary. It is often why campaign promises are vague—in large part to account for that flexibility to avoid necessarily sticking to that specific path. That said, while there is nothing wrong with building the ability to innovate and develop a plan along the way, when the foundational intention becomes diluted by countless exterior factors, a plan's fundamental impact very often goes by the wayside. Arguably this is what happened to President Lincoln's Reconstruction; his vision was as grand as the monument that bears his name, but after his death, the plan's caregivers modified and compromised its objectives until they were unrecognizable from the original intent.

In 1861, four million Black people were in slavery in America.[8] Following the Emancipation Proclamation of 1863 and by the end of the Civil War, the Confederacy fell and an amendment to the Constitution technically freed these slaves. While the ultimate question was how to rebuild and integrate the Confederate states back into the Union, some people looked beyond the idea of just restoring the rebel states and pondered how Black people and poor Southern Whites could become part of and be empowered by the new society.[9] More questions and virtually no answers were available to these impacted communities in the wake of Confederate General Robert E. Lee's surrender at the Appomattox Court House to the Union forces of General Ulysses S. Grant, a surrender that the Confederacy would present not as a victory of principle, but rather as a victory simply because the Union had more soldiers.[10]

Lincoln's concept of transitioning Black people from slavery required deciding what would be next for the freed slaves. One thought was deporting the slaves from the United States.[11] In 1862, Lincoln brought together Black spiritual leaders to gauge their reaction to this approach. The leaders vehemently opposed this proposal, as Black people had been in the United States for generations. Famed abolitionist Harriet Tubman had conveyed this sentiment in 1859, stating, "They can't do it; we're rooted here, and they can't pull us up."[12] After much work by abolitionists, Black clergy, and Black journalists, Lincoln changed his approach within one month.[13] On New Year's Eve in 1862, Black churchgoers in the North—including Frederick Douglass and Harriet Beecher Stowe—gathered to pray and sing for the delivery of the Emancipation Proclamation, which

---

[8]   *Reconstruction: America After the Civil War*, directed by Julia Marchesi (PBS, 2019).

[9]   *Reconstruction: America After the Civil War*.

[10]   *Reconstruction: America After the Civil War*.

[11]   H. L. Gates, *The Black Church* (Penguin Books, 2021), 65.

[12]   Gates, *The Black Church*, 65.

[13]   Gates, *The Black Church*, 65.

did not ultimately reference deportation and did support Black participation in the Union army. This led almost two hundred thousand Black
men to join the fight to restore the Union and end slavery for all.[14]

Reconstruction technically lasted from 1865 to 1877 and promised
to bind the nation back together both socially and economically. Its
failures have been well documented, with one observer noting that the
Reconstruction period left every American with something to regret.[15] It
was originally intended to promote a geographical unity that would refed-
eralize and at the same time heal the country, as evidenced by Lincoln's
1863 public reference to "Amnesty and Reconstruction," a plan that
would recognize pardons and support harmonizing the South and the
Union.[16] Some of Lincoln's fellow Republicans supported this effort, as it
could play a role in ending both the war and slavery, while others became
particularly critical of any approach that would set forth any clemency
for secessionists.[17] Assuming that problem could be addressed, the glaring

---

[14] Gates, *The Black Church*, 67.
[15] *Reconstruction: America After the Civil War.*
[16] *"By this point in the Civil War, it was clear that Lincoln needed to make some
      preliminary plans for postwar reconstruction. The Union armies had captured
      large sections of the South, and some states were ready to have their governments
      rebuilt. The proclamation addressed three main areas of concern. First, it al-
      lowed for a full pardon for and restoration of property to all engaged in the rebel-
      lion with the exception of the highest Confederate officials and military leaders.
      Second, it allowed for a new state government to be formed when 10 percent of
      the eligible voters had taken an oath of allegiance to the United States. Third, the
      Southern states admitted in this fashion were encouraged to enact plans to deal
      with the formerly enslaved people so long as their freedom was not compromised."*
      "President Lincoln Issues Proclamation of Amnesty and Reconstruction,"
      History Channel, https://www.history.com/this-day-in-history/lincoln-issues-
      proclamation-of-amnesty-and-reconstruction.
[17] *"In short, the terms of the plan were easy for most Southerners to accept. Though
      the emancipation of enslaved people was an impossible pill for some Confederates to
      swallow, Lincoln's plan was charitable, considering the costliness of the war. With
      the Proclamation of Amnesty and Reconstruction, Lincoln was seizing the initiative*

issue that remained was how the country could incorporate freed slaves into its daily fabric—including basic components of civil society that many take for granted today, such as literacy, education, bank accounts, job training, and employment agreements.

The political realities of the day affected these matters. The Emancipation Proclamation and the Thirteenth Amendment freed the slaves but did not speak to their right to vote. That said, these actions did begin to give the South a technical electoral advantage now that each slave would be counted as a full member of the state's population, as opposed to the previous three-fifths compromise, which had been used to determine congressional representation.[18] Without a vote, a realistic political strategy was for Southern Democrats to take control of Congress and implement policies that benefited them and their party—much of which would ironically be due to the freedoms that Republicans such as Lincoln sought to achieve.[19] This political reality was not lost on Lincoln—who, out of morality or political necessity, dedicated his last public speech on April 11,

---

for reconstruction from Congress. Some Radical Republicans thought the plan was far too easy on the South, but others accepted it because of the president's prestige and leadership. Following Lincoln's assassination in April 1865, the disagreements over the postwar reconstruction policy led to a heated battle between the next president, Andrew Johnson, and Congress." "President Lincoln Issues Proclamation of Amnesty and Reconstruction."

[18] "*Emancipation enhanced the South's share of national power by propelling 3.9 million former slaves into the ranks of the population used as a basis for apportionment. With slavery gone, each former bondsperson would now be counted as a whole person rather than three-fifths of one. In principle, this was a "5/5" scenario, in which all people (former slaves among them) were considered for purposes of representation.*" Patrick Rael, "Did Disenfranchisement Give the South an Electoral Advantage? *Journal of the Civil War Era* (December 13, 2016), https://www.journalofthecivilwarera.org/2016/12/disenfranchisement-give-south-electoral-advantage/.

[19] "*In the 1872 election cycle, which was the first to rely on post-emancipation census figures, the South controlled 138 of 366 (38 percent) EV. Had former slaves not been included (a "0/5" scenario), the South would have controlled only 90 of 319 (29 percent) EV. The emancipated freedpeople thus gave the South a 9 percent bump*

1865, to the beginning of extending the vote to Black people.[20] Referring back to his own second inauguration speech with his famous line about "malice towards none," Lincoln coupled this desire to do the right thing for Black people with preserving the entirety of the nation, including allowing the former Confederates access to economic opportunities.[21]

It is fair to say that Lincoln was conducting a delicate dance at this pivotal moment in history, as he was balancing the maintenance of the Union with the larger natural rights of mankind.[22] One anecdote in particular describes how Frederick Douglass was dismayed upon hearing that

---

in representation in the Electoral College." Rael, "Did Disenfranchisement Give the South an Electoral Advantage?"

[20] *"These twelve thousand persons [Louisiana voters] are thus fully committed to the Union, and to perpetual freedom in the state—committed to the very things, and nearly all the things the nation wants—and they ask the nations recognition and it's assistance to make good their committal. Now, if we reject, and spurn them, we do our utmost to disorganize and disperse them. We in effect say to the white men 'You are worthless, or worse—we will neither help you, nor be helped by you.' To the blacks we say 'This cup of liberty which these, your old masters, hold to your lips, we will dash from you, and leave you to the chances of gathering the spilled and scattered contents in some vague and undefined when, where, and how.'"* Abraham Lincoln's last public address, April 11, 1865, http://www.abrahamlincolnonline. org/lincoln/speeches/last.htm.

[21] *"With malice toward none with charity for all with firmness in the right as God gives us to see the right let us strive on to finish the work we are in to bind up the nation's wounds, to care for him who shall have borne the battle and for his widow and his orphan - to do all which may achieve and cherish a just and lasting peace among ourselves and with all nations."* Neely Tucker, "Inauguration Stories: Lincoln's 1865 'With Malice Toward None' Speech," Library of Congress, January 21, 2021, https://blogs.loc.gov/loc/2021/01/ inauguration-stories-lincolns-1865-with-malice-toward-none-speech/.

[22] *"After concluding with the strange warning that he [Lincoln] might be on the verge of making 'some new announcement to the people of the South,' Lincoln withdrew, leaving many in the audience disappointed. The speech wouldn't go over well with Lincoln's critics, either: Senator Charles Sumner of Massachusetts, the leading Radical, claimed the president was only promoting 'confusion and uncertainty in the future—with hot controversy.'"* Sarah Pruitt, "What Lincoln Said In His Final

Lincoln was essentially supporting suffrage only for Black veterans of the war and for those who were literate, but then how Douglass ultimately took comfort in the idea that this strategy was informed by the political acumen that Lincoln had developed over his career. Douglass recognized that Lincoln was a rail splitter, and knew that starting with the thin edge of the wedge can ultimately break apart the object at hand.[23]

While Lincoln publicly commented on the ills of slavery in both his legal and state legislative lives,[24] much of his focus was on economics and not necessarily race.[25] As would come to be seen, he went through a number of iterations of how the United States would look after the war, and while his outlook on slavery was ultimately clear, he always maintained a practical economic view of what would happen once peace was made. Part of his view was evidenced by the free-labor ideology, which concentrated on the dignity of the actual labor itself, as opposed to it being conducted by slaves.[26] This translated into support for an ecosystem of small business owners, such as farmers and skilled craftsmen.[27] For Lincoln, beyond just the inhumanity of slavery, he saw the practice as denying men and women basic economic prosperity from the fruits of their labor.[28] In fact, in his famous debates with Stephen Douglas in 1858, he referred to slavery as part of the "tyrannical principle," saying, "It is the same spirit that says, 'You work and toil and earn bread, and I'll eat it.'"[29]

Speech," History Channel, August 31, 2018, https://www.history.com/news/what-lincoln-said-in-his-final-speech.

[23] "Frederick Douglass, Abraham Lincoln, and the Contentious Path to Emancipation," *History Unplugged Podcast*.

[24] "Frederick Douglass, Abraham Lincoln, and the Contentious Path to Emancipation."

[25] J. Rodrigue, *Lincoln and Reconstruction* (Southern Illinois University Press, 2013), 5.

[26] Rodrigue, *Lincoln and Reconstruction*, 9.

[27] Rodrigue, *Lincoln and Reconstruction*, 9.

[28] Rodrigue, *Lincoln and Reconstruction*, 10.

[29] Rodrigue, *Lincoln and Reconstruction*, 9.

Lincoln identified the concept of Reconstruction as "the greatest question ever presented to practical statesmanship," showing that the economic question was always at the forefront of policy, and implying that an implementable plan had seemingly evaded policy makers up to that time.[30] One author poses that Lincoln's mindset developed over time, changing its focus from simply winning the war to contemplating first the fate of the democratic government, then the idealistic meaning of the American experiment, and finally the transcendent progress of mankind.[31] In an 1861 speech before Congress, Lincoln stated that the Civil War was "a struggle for maintaining in the world, that form, and substance of government, whose leading object is, to elevate the condition of men—to lift artificial weights from all shoulders—to clear paths of laudable pursuit for all—to afford all, an unfettered start, and a fair chance, in the race of life."[32] This approach firmly positioned his thinking on the matter, and not unlike George Washington and Benjamin Franklin had done before him with France, Lincoln used this broad humanitarian philosophy perhaps not only to make a global statement but also to practically persuade other countries like Great Britain not to support the Confederacy and instead to recognize the morality of this fight.[33]

For Lincoln, his vision truly became one that would reconstruct the Union as something of a new nation with a new national identity—as opposed to a nation that would simply be restored to the way it was before the war.[34] But the physical embodiment of that became difficult to imagine, as he stated before his death that "there is no authorized organ for us to treat with.... We simply must begin with, and mold from disor-

---

[30] Rodrigue, *Lincoln and Reconstruction*, 12
[31] Rodrigue, *Lincoln and Reconstruction*, 54–55.
[32] Rodrigue, *Lincoln and Reconstruction*, 55.
[33] Rodrigue, *Lincoln and Reconstruction*, 55.
[34] Rodrigue, *Lincoln and Reconstruction*, 66.

ganized and discordant elements."[35] You see, the country—and arguably many other societies over the course of history—had never undergone a self-examination to determine how it could support and essentially re-incorporate an entire people into its world. Before this time, Americans had gone from being early settlers to being revolutionaries to being the pioneers of Western expansion. Not unlike today, Americans looked to their leaders to provide some kind of blueprint to follow.

On April 15, 1865, all hope for such a tangible blueprint died with Lincoln's assassination. On that fateful day, his plan to simultaneously heal and transform the country transferred to his vice president, and now president, Andrew Johnson. President Johnson can usually be found near the bottom of the list of U.S. presidential rankings; however, from a legacy perspective, his inaction during this period would serve to prove impactful and a key reason for the failure of Reconstruction's promise of true equality. In fact, Johnson, a Tennessee Democrat who left a Senate seat in opposition to secession, found his way onto Lincoln's ticket just so Lincoln could show some goodwill toward the intended reunification of the country.[36] He undoubtedly had personal failings as a man—alleged to have been drunk at his own inauguration—but his focus in the early days of Reconstruction was to exact a vengeance on the Southern states, a position that stemmed from his belief that the Civil War had been fought for the benefit of the Southern planter class, who had looked down on poor Whites like him since he was a boy.[37] Ultimately, Johnson announced his plan for Reconstruction, which eventually provided amnesty to most White Southerners. But interestingly enough, as an act of almost individual vengeance, he required almost all of the Southern plantation

---

[35] Rodrigue, *Lincoln and Reconstruction*, 137.
[36] A. Guelzo, *Reconstruction: A Concise History* (Oxford University Press, 2018), 15–16.
[37] *Reconstruction: America After the Civil War.*

owners to come to him personally and request a pardon, a gesture that undoubtedly addressed his own childhood traumas and treatment.[38]

That said, President Johnson took some milquetoast measures to promote the concept of Reconstruction, and his economic policies began to resuscitate the South as he began rolling back some trading restrictions and certain port blockades throughout the region.[39] The man appointed to lead much of the actual Reconstruction effort was Major General Oliver Otis Howard, as commissioner of the Bureau of Refugees, Freedmen and Abandoned Lands, which would more famously become known as the Freedmen's Bureau. Major General Howard, a well-regarded man and an eventual founder of famed Howard University, was given the responsibility of overseeing the social and economic efforts to integrate the Black community by using funds from confiscated Confederate lands to develop plans for programs to support education, workforce opportunity, and civil society.[40] The Freedmen's Bureau was not necessarily there specifically to protect people, but rather to ensure fair and equitable relations,[41] and its annual budget has been described as not much more than the cost of a day of fighting the Civil War.[42] It oversaw huge land grants by the federal government, and those land grants were intended to set the stage for the development of an agrarian economy that would support and sustain an eventual upward mobility for the former slaves.[43] However, just as with many of President Johnson's other actions, his intentions became apparent when he ordered the return of many prop-

---

[38] *Reconstruction: America After the Civil War.*
[39] *Reconstruction: America After the Civil War.*
[40] Guelzo, *Reconstruction: A Concise History,* 20.
[41] *"Disturbed by the 'small, endless, mean little injustice of every day, Otis Howard created a system of bureau courts to handle magistrate-level cases—and thereby take them out of the hands of Southern civil courts."* Guelzo, *Reconstruction: A Concise History,* 32.
[42] *Reconstruction: America After the Civil War.*
[43] *Reconstruction: America After the Civil War.*

erties to the pardoned Southerners—significantly impacting what the Freedmen's Bureau could achieve.[44] In short, Johnson's Reconstruction ostensibly included the end of slavery—although forms of indentured servitude would remain—and that was about it. And at the time, not much more could be done to combat that approach on a legislative level, as Congress was in recess until December of 1865.[45]

President Johnson's intransigence can be directly linked to modern America's lack of economic mobility.[46] Putting aside the psychological reasons why he did what he did, from a policy perspective, it is not so difficult to draw a line from that moment to many of today's social and economic disparities. Further, Johnson's approach intentionally included steps that hindered structural changes. For example, he appointed former secessionists to meaningful political roles, and this, coupled with the election of pardoned Southerners, produced an antagonistic legal framework in the application of civil rights.[47] These circumstances eventually led to the Black Codes, a series of state and local ordinances that served to limit free speech and employment opportunities for the freedmen, as well as their ability to own firearms—which of course impacted their ability to combat any associated violence against them.[48] Another example of

---

[44] *Reconstruction: America After the Civil War.*

[45] *Reconstruction: America After the Civil War.*

[46] *Reconstruction: America After the Civil War.*

[47] *"President Johnson implemented his own reconstruction plan during the summer of 1865. Eager to include Southern states, he appointed provisional governors, many of whom were former Confederates, and empowered them to call state constitutional conventions. After ratifying new constitutions and electing new state governments, Johnson promised that the states could regain full federal recognition within the Union."* "The Civil War: The Senate's Story: Victory, Tragedy, and Reconstruction, Union Victory and National Tragedy," United States Senate, https://www.senate.gov/artandhistory/history/common/civil_war/VictoryTragedyReconstruction.htm.

[48] *"After the Civil War, the Black Codes enacted in the South made it a crime for a Black person to have a gun."* Adam Winkler, "Racism and the Second

limiting legislation was the so-called vagrancy laws, which impacted Black people who did not sign a labor contract with a White employer. Such individuals were deemed to be vagrants, and could be arrested and auctioned off to someone for whom they would perform labor services, with minimal compensation.[49] Further, Black people who did not have a job could have their children taken away, as they were determined to be indigent. Those children could be acquired by others and taught to farm and clean, under the guise of apprenticeship.[50] In some places, schools were forbidden, former slaves were unable to travel without proper paperwork from former owners, and others were driven away from farms after completing their own harvest.[51] Frederick Douglass noted that while slavery may have been outlawed, the local laws and their execution were creating a new kind of bondage for Black people.[52]

Ultimately, President Johnson lost control of these circumstances—which, coupled with pushback from leaders in the Northern states, led folks to wonder whether a new civil war could happen. At the start of the new Congress in December 1865, although Johnson had called for the end of Reconstruction, his Republican opponents developed a strategy to advance significant reform, which began with not swearing in any representatives of the former Confederacy.[53] These newly elected congressmen from the South included the former vice president of the Confederacy, several Confederate generals, and other high-ranking Confederate officials. If permitted to sit in Congress, these representatives could lead an effort to shut down Reconstruction in all its forms. Driven by what he referred to as a "moral obligation to create freedom," Republican Senator Thaddeus Stevens oversaw a strategy to simply not seat these

---

Amendment," *Harvard Law Review* (June 21, 2022), 1.

49 *Reconstruction: America After the Civil War.*
50 *Reconstruction: America After the Civil War.*
51 *Reconstruction: America After the Civil War.*
52 *Reconstruction: America After the Civil War.*
53 *Reconstruction: America After the Civil War.*

newly elected officials, by ensuring that the congressional clerk did not call their names, as having one's name called was an administrative requirement of congressional membership.[54] With that, Senator Stevens and his Republican colleagues greatly outnumbered the Democrats and established a swift and significant legislative agenda as a direct response to the Black Codes. In April, they passed the Civil Rights Act of 1866, which established birthright citizenship to all—including Black people.[55] The Republican agenda also included efforts to allow for certain state voting bills for freed slaves, and for the extension of the Freedmen's Bureau beyond its initial year of establishment.[56]

The circumstances under which that extension occurred were tied to the fact that Major General Howard, as leader of the Freedmen's Bureau, sought to remove matters from local courts in the South to avoid bias and

---

[54] *Reconstruction: America After the Civil War. See also The Civil War: The Senate's Story: Victory, Tragedy, and Reconstruction, Union Victory and National Tragedy,* United States Senate, https://www.senate.gov/artandhistory/history/common/ civil_war/VictoryTragedyReconstruction.htm, *"When the 39th Congress convened on December 4, 1865, some of the newly elected legislators from former Confederate states presented credentials, expecting to be seated in the Senate. Questions about the validity of the credentials prompted the House and Senate to establish a Joint Committee on Reconstruction. This 15-member committee, composed of 9 representatives and 6 senators, investigated 'the conditions of the States which formed the so-called confederate States of America' to determine whether they 'are entitled to be represented in either House of Congress.' Following its investigation, the committee refused to admit the Southern members."*

[55] *Reconstruction: America After the Civil War.*

[56] *"The issue floundered until May, when a more moderate House bill to extend the Freedmen's Bureau was proposed. This final bill gained approval by both the House and the Senate and went to the president on July 3. Again, President Johnson vetoed the bill. This time, however, both the Senate and the House mustered the two-thirds majorities necessary to override the veto. The Freedmen's Bureau Act of 1866 became law on July 16, extending the work of the agency for two more years."* "Freedmen's Bureau Acts of 1865 and 1866," United States Senate, https://www.senate.gov/ artandhistory/history/common/generic/FreedmensBureau.htm.

advance the institution's stated goals.[57] President Johnson saw some of these actions as contradicting the property rights that he sought to sustain for the secessionists. As such, he vetoed the Freedmen's Bureau Bill in July 1866, but that veto ultimately was overridden by the Republicans in Congress. Johnson's public rationale for his veto was that the extension of the Freedmen's Bureau was in fact illegal, as wartime authorities were no longer in effect.[58] Johnson also vetoed the Republicans' Civil Rights Bill of 1866, but the Republicans overrode that as well. Notably, the Civil Rights Bill laid the foundation for the Fourteenth Amendment, which would provide Black people with citizenship and equal protection under the laws.[59]

The Republicans wanted to make an undeniable statement that they were in charge, and set forth a plan that for the former Confederate states to be readmitted to the Union and have their representatives hold seats in Congress, they must ratify the Fourteenth Amendment, write new state constitutions that reflected the desired societal changes, and hold new elections while giving Black men the right to vote and hold office.[60] This

---

[57] *"Disturbed by the 'small, endless, mean little injustice of every day, Otis Howard created a system of bureau courts to handle magistrate-level cases—and thereby take them out of the hands of Southern civil courts."* Guelzo, *Reconstruction: A Concise History*, 32.

[58] *"Johnson's stated reasons for opposing the legislation were similar to the arguments made by the measure's opponents in the House and Senate—it was unnecessary to extend the original legislation, it infringed on states' rights, it gave the federal government an unprecedented role in providing aid to a specific group of people at the exclusion of others, and it was expensive. Johnson had resisted all congressionally driven reconstruction programs and denounced those who stood 'opposed to the restoration of the Union.' He viewed the Southern states as fully restored and thus 'entitled to enjoy their constitutional rights as members of the Union.'"* "Freedmen's Bureau Acts of 1865 and 1866."

[59] "14th Amendment to the U.S. Constitution: Civil Rights (1868)," https://www. archives.gov/milestone-documents/14th-amendment.

[60] *Reconstruction: America After the Civil War.*

led to massive voter registration for Black men as their voting population went from 1 percent to 80 percent.[61]

The Republicans' efforts also led to an age of significant public engagement for Black people, during which they embraced their new civic responsibilities and met regularly to debate the Constitution and develop their place in this new society, with some walking over twenty miles to participate in these important discussions.[62] Churches became the cornerstones of the Black community during Reconstruction, as they hosted these meetings and provided educational opportunities.[63] In fact, one Reconstruction academic has stated that "to tell the story of American religion is to tell a political story."[64] Over time, state legislatures and private philanthropists would fill this educational need, establishing schools, public hospitals, and other social systems in Southern states—many of which involved Black elected leaders.[65] These school systems needed teachers, and the foundations of the historically black college and university system developed to advance literacy as a foundational component of economic mobility for these former slaves.[66] Alongside these changes, Black office holders emerged at all levels, including in the very important local positions of judges and justices of the peace, through which they sought to ensure a fair process and order during these civic and social transitions.[67]

It is important to underscore the incredible importance of the Black church in these efforts. In his book *The Black Church*, Harvard University professor Henry Louis Gates Jr. identifies this community as "a cultural

---

[61]   *Reconstruction: America After the Civil War.*
[62]   *Reconstruction: America After the Civil War.*
[63]   *Reconstruction: America After the Civil War.*
[64]   Gates, *The Black Church*, 56.
[65]   *Reconstruction: America After the Civil War.*
[66]   *Reconstruction: America After the Civil War.*
[67]   *Reconstruction: America After the Civil War.*

system…of symbols and signs. And navigating its multiple levels and nebulous contours demanded a sophisticated degree of cultural literacy, the training for which began in Sunday school, ranging from ways to dress and comport oneself…"[68] Gates also makes the point that the Black church was no single religion, but rather a number of identified faiths that brought slaves and freedmen together for both religious and secular matters—and, just as importantly, permitted a dialogue on social and economic life to occur in somewhat secure locations.[69] This range of worship included the African Methodist Episcopal Church (AME), the AME Zion Church, the National Baptist Convention (NBC), the Catholic Church, and the Church of God in Christ (COGIC).[70] It was the safety of these venues that in part allowed for the fueling of rebellions and the establishment of massive endeavors such as the Underground Railroad.[71] The biblical passages around the exodus of the Israelites supported generations of Black slaves; the words were not merely aspirational but literally spoke to a people in bondage.[72]

We see the beginnings of abolitionist support within these churches during a period in the 1730s known as the First Great Awakening. Black and White congregants worshipped openly and demonstratively next to each other, and participants provided testimonials about their experience—which also led to a rise in Black pastors whose congregations would openly vocalize their agreement with the pastors' preachings.[73] The Methodist Church grew in number due to its first public statement of opposition to slavery,[74] with the AME and AME Zion Churches providing opportunities for Black preachers and providing inspiration

---

[68] Gates, *The Black Church*, xxii.
[69] Gates, *The Black Church*, 1–3.
[70] Gates, *The Black Church*, 9–10.
[71] Gates, *The Black Church*, 5.
[72] Gates, *The Black Church*, 35.
[73] Gates, *The Black Church*, 41.
[74] Gates, *The Black Church*, 46.

for famed abolitionists such as Sojourner Truth, Harriet Tubman, and Frederick Douglass.[75]

Of additional importance is how the preachers not only led these congregations but also became publicly identified as social leaders. An early example of this was when Union General William Tecumseh Sherman and U.S. Secretary of War Edwin Stanton met with leaders of the Black community in January 1865 in Savannah, Georgia, to discuss the future of Black refugees. In that meeting, it was Black preacher Garrison Frazier who secured the redistribution of lands under the Sherman Land Act of 1865, an approach that—until President Johnson—would help the North develop opportunities for the freedmen in the deep South.[76] In fact, settling these areas gave these Black communities the opportunity to build churches for both worship and educational support, as well as build homes. It is noteworthy that often the first item to be situated in these new homes was a Bible, so that the residents could ensure that they could advance their understanding of the scripture as much as possible in order to follow the words and lessons of their particular pastor.[77] These lessons and the educational programs that developed in church basements were the early precursors to HBCUs.[78] And Black preachers would become members of elected office and leaders of social change during a period that has been referred to as the Second Reconstruction.[79] This period culminated in the civil rights movement of the 1950s and 1960s with Dr. Martin Luther King Jr., who was himself an heir to this legacy as the son of a preacher of the Ebenezer Baptist Church in Atlanta.

In the spring of 1867, Congress continued to pass Reconstruction laws to support the freedmen, and later that year, President Johnson

---

[75]   Gates, *The Black Church*, 48–49.
[76]   Gates, *The Black Church*, 74–75.
[77]   Gates, *The Black Church*, 82.
[78]   Gates, *The Black Church*, 82.
[79]   Gates, *The Black Church*, 131.

became embroiled in his own impeachment after his violation of the Tenure of Office Act. This circumstance rested on the allegation that he sought to undermine his Department of War's efforts to advance Reconstruction activities, ultimately leading to the resignation of General Ulysses S. Grant from the Johnson administration, setting the stage for Grant's own track to the White House. What Johnson had envisioned as simply a way to reincorporate the country, the Republicans turned into a massive plan for equality—but one that came at a significant cost. Race riots developed across the South, and it was at this time that the Ku Klux Klan (KKK) began to engage in open hostility, intimidation, and violence against Southern Black people, as well as against any White people who supported their cause.[80]

In 1868, the country elected a man to the presidency who didn't want the office, but rather saw it as a dutiful continuation of the work that he and President Lincoln had started. President Ulysses S. Grant was known as the "Hero of Appomattox," and his voters sought to usher in a leader who would advance reforms on behalf of Black people, and do so in a way that would codify these changes as part of the lawful fabric of the country. But Grant also knew that the country could not survive another war, and that maintaining the peace was critical to his plan's success. Among his supporters was Frederick Douglass, who saw Grant, a Republican, as a champion with both the knowledge and the standing to navigate these waters. Douglass famously stated that "the Republican party is the ship and all else is the sea."[81]

---

[80] *"Founded in 1866 as a Tennessee social club, the Ku Klux Klan [sic] now spread into nearly every Southern state, launching a 'reign of terror' against Republican leaders black and white."* Eric Foner, *Reconstruction: America's Unfinished Revolution, 1863-1877* (HarperCollins, 1988), 342. See also *Reconstruction: America After the Civil War.*

[81] *"After the 15th Amendment was passed in 1870 allowing most of the black males in the former Confederate states to vote, the Republican Party (also now known as the Grand Old Party or GOP) commanded the loyalty of an overwhelming majority*

The Fourteenth Amendment was finally ratified in July 1868, and the Fifteenth Amendment, which secured Black suffrage, was passed and sent to the states for ratification in February 1869. By the end of 1870, the remaining Southern states were all readmitted to the Union, which ultimately allowed the Democratic party to significantly dilute the Republican voting base, as well as engage in de facto racist policies that significantly pushed back on gains made by Black people after the Civil War.[82] These actions were coupled with the ongoing rise of the KKK, which became even more violent, continuing their destruction and murder throughout the South, including lynchings, which served to send a message to any that would oppose the openly racist policies.[83]

President Grant called upon his military background and his recently developed legislative policy skills to pass the Ku Klux Klan Act of 1871, which served to protect the community and thwart the KKK through the resources of the federal government.[84] This legislation led to arrests and prosecutions that would sustain the vision of Reconstruction that Grant

---

of African Americas, prompting Frederick Douglass to remark that for them, 'The Republican Party was the ship and all else was the sea.'" Ryan Byarlay, "Black and Tan Republicans," BlackPast, May 10, 2009, https://www.blackpast.org/african-american-history/black-and-tan-republicans/.

82 *Reconstruction: America After the Civil War.*

83 *Reconstruction: America After the Civil War.*

84 *"The House approved 'An Act to enforce the Provisions of the Fourteenth Amendment to the Constitution of the United States, and for other Purposes, also known as the 'Ku Klux Klan Act.' Introduced as H.R. 320 on March 28, 1871, by Representative Samuel Shellabarger of Ohio, the bill passed the House on April 6 and returned from the Senate with amendments on April 14. After nearly a week of heated debate in the House and the Senate, the chambers reconciled their differences on April 20 when the House agreed to the conference report on H.R. 320 and the Senate concurred. The Ku Klux Klan Act, the third of a series of increasingly stringent Enforcement Acts, was designed to eliminate extralegal violence and protect the civil and political rights of four million freed slaves."* "Ku Klux Klan Act of 1871," https://history.house.gov/Historical-Highlights/1851-1900/hh_1871_04_20_KKK_Act/.

sought to secure for his former commander-in-chief. Additional legislation addressed Reconstruction-era changes; for instance, the Republican
Congress established the Civil Rights Act of 1875, which prohibited
segregation for public facilities. This would stand until 1883, when it was
struck down by the U.S. Supreme Court in the *Plessy v. Ferguson* case,[85]
which would eventually be reversed by the Supreme Court case *Brown
v. Board of Education* in 1954. Thurgood Marshall, then counsel for the
National Association for the Advancement of Colored People (NAACP),
closed out his argument in the *Brown* case with the following important
words: "The only thing can be is an inherent determination that the
people who were formerly in slavery, regardless of anything else, shall be
kept as near that stage as is possible, and now is the time, we submit, that
this Court should make it clear that that is not what our Constitution
stands for."[86] Marshall would go on to be the nation's first Black Supreme
Court justice.

While the executive powers and responsibilities provided to him by
the Constitution served as President Grant's North Star during his tenure,
his two terms in office and a flurry of significant legislation to support
the cause of Black people were not enough to overcome the economic
impacts of the war, the strength of the Democratic party in the South,
and multiple stories of corruption within his own administration—all
of which hampered the Republicans' ability to hold to the path of the

---

[85] *"The case stemmed from an 1892 incident in which African American train pas-
senger Homer Plessy refused to sit in a car for Black people. Rejecting Plessy's
argument that his constitutional rights were violated, the Supreme Court ruled
that a law that "implies merely a legal distinction" between white people and
Black people was not unconstitutional. As a result, restrictive Jim Crow legislation
and separate public accommodations based on race became commonplace." Plessy
v. Ferguson* (1896), https://www.history.com/topics/black-history/plessy-v-fer-
guson#:~:text=Sources-,Plessy%20v.,a%20car%20for%20Black%20
people.

[86] *Brown v. Board of Education*, U.S. Supreme Court Transcript (1954), https://
www.loc.gov/item/usrep347483/.

Reconstruction that they had envisioned. By the end of this period, Black people were free, Black men could vote, and some HBCUs had been developed. However, economic mobility took a huge hit, as sharecropping in the South became commonplace. This practice allowed former slaves to work the land, but only as renters—and the rent prices often significantly impacted any profits they could reasonably earn.[87] After Grant's time in office, lynchings would peak in the 1890s, and the concepts of poll taxes and literacy tests would become routine at the voting booth—suppressing both the Black vote and the poor White vote.[88]

Still, the legacy of that period included clear progress on a number of fronts. Emancipation. Birthright citizenship. Voting rights. The KKK Act. Freedmen's schools and the early days of HBCUs. And while some ideas did not survive, others laid the groundwork for the possibilities to be discussed herein, as exemplified by the Freedman's Savings and Trust Company, which was more commonly known as the Freedman's Bank.[89] It was chartered in March 1865 as a banking structure for former slaves, and ultimately handled deposits of over $75 million.[90] The bank eventually expanded to thirty-five branches across the Southeast, with over seventy-five thousand depositors.[91]

---

[87]   *Reconstruction: America After the Civil War.*

[88]   *Reconstruction: America After the Civil War.*

[89]   *"… John W Alvord [founder], an abolitionist minister and army chaplain, encouraged Congress to use these funds [$200,000 in unclaimed bank dollars] to incorporate a bank for freed blacks in conjunction with the Freedmen's Bureau. The bill [approved by Congress and signed by President Lincoln on March 3, 1865] passed without opposition and was championed by reformer like Sumner and Alvord, neither of whom had any experience with finance or banking."* Mehrsa Baradaran, *The Color of Money* (The Belknap Press of Harvard University Press, 2017), 23.

[90]   Baradaran, *The Color of Money*, 25.

[91]   Baradaran, *The Color of Money*, 25.

Frederick Douglass became president of the Freedman's Bank during its later troubled times, providing it with a loan of $10,000.[92] He conveyed concerns of the bank's viability to Congress, and its doors were closed in 1874 due to mismanagement and fraud.[93] However, almost more important, its failure created a mistrust of financial institutions that was passed down to many generations of Black Americans—a mistrust that would become readily apparent almost one hundred and fifty years later during the COVID pandemic.[94] Today, there are only a handful of Black banks to carry on the lineage of the Freedman's Bank, and it is commonly held that part of the limited use of the federal government's Paycheck Protection Program by minorities during the COVID pandemic ties back to this generational mistrust of institutional banks. The identification of these issues and potential solutions for consideration gets to the heart of what this book seeks to achieve.

---

[92] *"Frederick Douglass celebrated the bank stating that the 'mission of the Freedmen's Bank is to show our people the road to a share of the wealth and well-being of the world.'" Reconstruction: America After the Civil War.* His appointment was not sought, nor did he have relevant experience, but the trustees appointed Douglass based on his reputation. *"Douglass quickly discovered that the bank was 'full of dead men's bones, rottenness and corruption.'"* See also Baradaran, *The Color of Money*, 23, 25, and 29.

[93] Baradaran, *The Color of Money*, 27, 30.

[94] *"So successful were the returns on speculation after 1867 that the bank initiated a propaganda campaign to draw out more deposits."* With management seeking to increase deposits by referring to land investment opportunities, they *advertised that land would mean "being your own master' and providing for your family.'* The advertisements also promised that *'there is no speculation and 'no risk in this Bank.'*... *[t]he bank managers began speculating in real estate and then, quite simply, a close ring of managers with unfettered discretion plundered the savings of the freedmen...* According to W.E.B. DuBois, *"what the bank eventually did... was 'not only ruine[d] thousands of colored men, but taught to thousands more a lesson of distrust which it will take them years to unlearn.'"* Baradaran, *The Color of Money*, 23, 27, and 28.

So what does it mean when the Republican party is referred to as "the party of Lincoln," and even more to the point, is that moniker still accurate? Technically, Abraham Lincoln was the first Republican president—or at least the first to be elected under the name of that party. He is often cited as the standard-bearer, but he was not a perfect man. He has been quoted as saying in September 1858 that he would not support Black suffrage, due to differences between White and Black men.[95] Of course this view would change over time, but nonetheless, it did exist at one point. But Lincoln evolved—a trait that is captured in his statement that he was "a slow walker but never walked backward."[96] Whether as a young attorney arguing before a jury or as an older statesman surveying a battlefield, he continually took steps that brought him closer to the reality he was facing. It was he—as a Republican—who led Emancipation. It was he—as a Republican—who started the road to universal suffrage, and society will always speculate as to what would have happened if this Republican had survived John Wilkes Booth's bullet. His successor, President Johnson, was unable to effectively lead due to his own history of racism, arrogance, inept stewardship, and seeming disregard for the entirety of what America aspires to be. President Grant picked up the mantle of Lincoln, but only where he could. His successes in universal suffrage

---

[95] *"I will say then that I am not, nor ever have been, in favor of bringing about in any way the social and political equality of the black and white races — that I am not nor ever have been in favor of making VOTERS or jurors of negroes, nor of qualifying them hold office, nor to intermarry with white people; and I will say in addition to this that there is a physical difference between the white and black races which I believe will forever forbid the two races living together on terms of social and political equality."* "Mr. Lincoln and Negro Equality," *The New York Times*, December 28, 1860, https://www.nytimes.com/1860/12/28/archives/mr-lincoln-and-negro-equality.html.

[96] Joseph McAuley, "'I Walk Slowly, But I Never Walk Backward': The Humanity of Abraham Lincoln," *America: The Jesuit Review*, February 15, 2015, https://www.americamagazine.org/politics-society/2015/02/15/i-walk-slowly-i-never-walk-backward-humanity-abraham-lincoln.

via the Fifteenth Amendment and the thrashing of the KKK were critical achievements for which he deserves significant credit, but he could not revive and complete Lincoln's intended vision for Reconstruction.

Is it fair to say that men like Lincoln, Grant, and Stevens laid the groundwork for the party of freedom and opportunity? The evidence suggests that the answer is yes. And why can that be said with such confidence? Because what makes politics work is the aspirational coupled with the intentional. And that is what Lincoln, Grant, and Stevens and the brave members of that Republican Congress did. This is what modern Republicans must aspire to be as a group of individuals committed to the advancement of all people. A skeptic may seek to criticize that position and point to contemporary political statements they deem to be inconsistent with that goal. And that criticism is the point of this book. Politics is one thing. Politics is composed of sound bites and stump speeches. Policy is different. It is the action-oriented plan that lays out what success can look like, and does so in a way that stays true to the party's principles. For Republicans, this means the principles set forth by Presidents Lincoln and Grant and supported by great leaders such as Frederick Douglass.

The objective is to create a truly civil society—or a community of citizens linked by common interests and collective activity.[97] That was the ultimate goal of Lincoln's vision of Reconstruction: that society would take on this mantle of progress because it was about the collective economic good. What has since happened is that some of society's most significant struggles have become isolated in different communities, and the federal government has taken the responsibility for those struggles from the community and sought to fill in the gaps as it sees fit—much of which has exacerbated the original problems. And this approach has become a constant in an equation that keeps weakening civil society. The next chapter will more deeply examine this problem as a market failure,

---

[97]   Nivar, "A Lost Generation and the Breakdown of (Civil) Society as We Know It."

demonstrating that capitalistic community solutions must be exercised for mutual benefit—and not in a way that seeks to unfairly take advantage of any particular community.

CHAPTER **THREE**

Underserved Communities as a Market Failure
and the Applicable Conservative Philosophy

Market failure has been defined as "the failure of a more or less idealized system of price-market institutions to sustain 'desirable' activities or to stop 'undesirable' activities."[98] Such failures can be addressed through either private or government solutions. Oftentimes, the market can be managed, but other times the challenge is so significant that the market must be supplemented in some fashion to sustain a level of acceptable performance. Whether it was expansive programs such as President Franklin Roosevelt's New Deal in the 1930s or efforts around the Great Recession of 2008, the federal government has consistently played a significant role in major events that have irreversibly impacted the trajectory of the country. While these efforts usually have been in response to a unique set of circumstances, such actions are often criticized

---

[98] Francis M. Bator, *The Theory of Market Failure, The Anatomy of Market Failure* (George Mason University Press, 1988), 35.

as antithetical to a pure market-based economy.[99] As an example, whatever one's position is on the individual components of the New Deal, a common modern-day conservative criticism of this initiative is that many of those programs have outlived their relevance, and have been administered in such a bureaucratic and untenable way that they have actually harmed the very same people they originally sought to help, by establishing a system of dependence.

Of course, to reach this conclusion, one must take the long view. It is easy for a politician to offer a sound bite on supporting *more* of any program, but it is quite another thing to examine actual data that results in generational perpetuation of the problem. The same politicians who disregard the facts and double down on these types of programs could very well be acting in their own self-interest, given that financial assistance to their communities might immediately result, but those politicians do not have to answer to the generations that follow. Their behavior is the epitome of inefficiency and irresponsibility, yet it has not only been permitted but actually encouraged for generations.

When examining how to address a decades-long market failure, the principle of "mutual benefit" should be considered. There is no mystery to this term other than that it describes a scenario in which both sides gain value. It is comparable to the underlying principle of capitalism, by which people on both sides of a transaction use the information they have available to them to engage in a contract that they have independently determined will provide them with the highest value. Ja'Ron often uses Dr. Martin Luther King Jr.'s analysis of capitalism to demonstrate this thinking. In a letter to his wife in 1952, King stated, "Imagine you already know that I am much more socialistic in my economic theory than capitalistic.... [Capitalism] started out with a noble and high motive...

---

[99] Ryan Bourne, "How 'Market Failure' Arguments Lead to Misguided Policy," Cato Institute, January 22, 2019, https://www.cato.org/policy-analysis/how-market-failure-arguments-lead-misguided-policy.

but like most human systems it fell victim to the very thing it was re-volting against. So today capitalism has out-lived its usefulness."[100] King expanded on this position in a speech to the Negro American Labor Council in 1961 when he said, "Call it democracy, or call it democratic socialism, but there must be a better distribution of wealth within this country for all God's children."[101] So, in short, King recognized that capitalism did have utility at one point, but posed that a different model for the distribution of wealth must ultimately be implemented.

With great respect to a man whose heroic legacy transcends American history, Ja'Ron disagrees with King on this point, arguing that the economic exploitation of Black people through slavery was inherently opposed to the concept of mutual benefit that underscores a capital-ist approach. Further, Ja'Ron argues that the concept of Economics of Mutuality created by the think tank Catalyst, an internal program of global food production company Mars led by chief economist Bruno Roach, is helpful in better understanding this debate.[102] Roach argues that "if a company invests in both non-financial and financial capital using standardized metrics within a broader ecosystem that includes all of its key stakeholders as well as its shareholders, not only does holistic value increase across the board, but the company's performance also improves."[103]

This concept was brought to Ja'Ron's attention during a meeting at the White House with one of Roach's colleagues, Jay Jakub, and he has since incorporated it into his work with underserved communities. The

[100] "Martin Luther King on Capitalism in His Own Words," MLK Global, November 23, 2017, https://mlkglobal.org/2017/11/23/martin-luther-king-on-capitalism-in-his-own-words/.

[101] "Martin Luther King on Capitalism in His Own Words."

[102] "Completing Capitalism: Transforming the Economic System by Creating a Mutuality of Benefits Among All Stakeholders," Economics of Mutuality, https://eom.org/.

[103] "Completing Capitalism."

philosophy expands on the uninformed model of merely distributing money that is so often utilized by large federal government programs, to rather embrace the concept of measuring success with data on performance and value creation, incorporating a constant examination of how private sector businesses and financial institutions can engage to advance a mutual benefit in society. When applied through this lens, this concept could redefine the conservatives' view of environmental, social, and corporate governance (ESG) for underserved communities.

To illustrate the negative aspects of merely distributing money, let us examine how massive federal government–led programs have led to enormously impactful unintended consequences. Take, for example, the New Deal's impact on what is commonly known as *redlining*. This term, which is synonymous with racial exclusion, found its origins in the New Deal agency the Home Owners' Loan Corporation (HOLC).[104] This agency established a color-coded map highlighting the country's most desirable places to live. As you might guess, the least desirable places were marked in red, and just happened to disproportionately be home to many Black Americans.[105] Once these maps were distributed to financial institutions, those areas became the least likely to receive home loans, leading to a limited ability for residents there to access the capital needed for economic mobility.[106] Was this the stated intention of the program? Presumably it was not, but it has impacted the national housing market for almost one hundred years, and its legacy continues to be a factor that activists point to in efforts to address housing inequality.[107] As famed

---

[104] "A Forgotten History of How Our Government Segregated America," *Fresh Air*, May 3, 2017, National Public Radio.

[105] "A Forgotten History of How Our Government Segregated America."

[106] *"This not only meant that blacks could not buy homes and build capital in the 'undesirable' inner city; it also meant that they were trapped in neighborhoods in rapid decline…"* Baradaran, *The Color of Money: Black Banks and the Racial Wealth Gap*, 105.

[107] "A Forgotten History of How Our Government Segregated America."

economist Milton Friedman stated, "Most of the energy of political work is devoted to correcting the effects of mismanagement of government,"[108] and redlining is clearly an example of such mismanagement.

While Reconstruction is recognized for presenting a framework for the North and the South to reengage as a single union, the failure to implement President Lincoln's sweeping vision has provided a lasting legacy for America. While both Black and poor Southern White people were unable to stand upon the pillar of possibility that was to be provided by Reconstruction, academics do underscore the fact that some advances were made—including significant increases in literacy and land ownership.[109] The negatives were compounded by widespread poverty and seemingly insurmountable civic limitations such as voting restrictions and segregation across almost all of public life. The collective result of slavery, attempted integration, and decades of failed policies have created something akin to a market failure, the horizon of which has only grown over time.

That said, the admirable work and notable successes of those who have sought to make a difference must be acknowledged and appreciated. For example, many scholars draw a line directly from Reconstruction to the civil rights movement, seeing the latter as an extension of unfinished work. While the civil rights movement and its brave leaders certainly concentrated on issues impacting the Black community, which led to massive positive societal changes, the movement also served as something of a platform for a number of disenfranchised groups, as it specifically highlighted the importance of economic mobility. In fact, the March on Washington in 1963 was intended in part as a rallying call for employment opportunities, and while King's speech certainly was the hallmark of that event, various remarks made that day specifically advocated for

---

[108] *Reconstruction: America After the Civil War.*
[109] *Reconstruction: America After the Civil War.*

widespread economic mobility. In fact, the march's full name was the March on Washington for Jobs and Freedom.[110]

Even with the historic constitutional amendments and other groundbreaking legislation, the period after the end of Reconstruction and into the beginning of the twentieth century (1877–1901), often called the "Nadir period," was one of the most violent toward Black people.[111] Rather than being about a foundational rise for Blacks, this period became more aligned with the reality that Northern support for civil rights had waned, in part due to the interest of avoiding yet another war.[112] While stories exist about pockets of Black communities that flourished economically for a time, such as "Black Wall Street" in Tulsa, Oklahoma,[113] violent murders, lynchings, and other attacks by the KKK reached historic levels during this period; and this violence was compounded by the de facto disenfranchising of Blacks through the Jim Crow laws.[114] The abandonment of President's Lincoln's vision, and the obvious trauma associated

---

[110] King Institute, "March on Washington for Jobs and Freedom," Stanford University, https://kinginstitute.stanford.edu/encyclopedia/march-washington-jobs-and-freedom.

[111] *Reconstruction: America After the Civil War.*

[112] *Reconstruction: America After the Civil War.*

[113] *"At the turn of the 20th century, the Greenwood District of Tulsa, Oklahoma, became one of the first communities in the country thriving with Black entrepreneurial businesses. The prosperous town, founded by many descendants of slaves, earned a reputation as the Black Wall Street of America and became a harbor for African Americans in a highly segregated city under Jim Crow laws. On May 31, 1921, a white mob turned Greenwood upside down in one of the worst racial massacres in U.S. history. In the matter of hours, 35 square blocks of the vibrant Black community were turned into smoldering ashes. Countless Black people were killed — estimates ranged from 55 to more than 300 — and 1,000 homes and businesses were looted and set on fire."* Yun Li, "Black Wall Street Was Shattered 100 Years Ago. How the Tulsa Race Massacre Was Covered Up and Unearthed," CNBC, May 31, 2021, https://www.cnbc.com/2021/05/31/black-wall-street-was-shattered-100-years-ago-how-tulsa-race-massacre-was-covered-up.html.

[114] *Reconstruction: America After the Civil War.*

with this violence and social upheaval, created a generational impact throughout the Black community whose effects can still be felt at both civic and familial levels today. Throughout this whole period, a resilient people made notable advancements, such as significant increases in home ownership, increased educational levels with the stability of HBCUs, and strengthened family households.[115] But these successes were achieved amid an onslaught of violence and civil relegation.[116]

During the first few decades of the 1900s and into the 1960s, identifiable—but certainly not expedient—progress had been made for the Black community. Neighborhood integration grew over time, and economic opportunities for Black professionals increased. Political significance grew under the leadership of Dr. King, and American leaders' focus on certain economic initiatives followed suit, as evidenced by President Richard Nixon's creation of the precursor to the U.S. Commerce Department's Minority Business Development Agency in 1969, which concentrates on small business and entrepreneurship initiatives for Black Americans and other minorities.[117] Even with this progress, however, racism remained very relevant in the United States, class structures persisted, and with a lack of mutual benefit openly applied to the circumstances, certain historic remnants of Reconstruction engendered a significant mistrust of the federal government by Black Americans that was handed down from generation to generation.

As mentioned, after the end of slavery, tenant farming—which closely resembled slave labor—became one of the most common work

---

[115] *Reconstruction: America After the Civil War.*

[116] *Reconstruction: America After the Civil War.*

[117] The Minority Business Development Agency (MBDA) was originally established as the Office of Minority Business Enterprise by President Richard M. Nixon on March 5, 1969, "The History of the MBDA," Minority Business Development Agency, https://www.mbda.gov/about/history.

opportunities for freedmen.[118] While many White people were competing in this tenant farmer space, some would eventually find opportunities in textile factories in the South. Eventually Black workers became part of the Southern textile industry as well, with the introduction of equal opportunity policy, a notion that was additionally advanced in a March 1961 executive order by President John Kennedy.[119] That executive order focused on the activities associated with defense contracts, and the development of fabric needs for the military presented significant opportunities for fabric manufacturing factories in North Carolina. Over time, textile executives realized that not only was this the law of the land, but the additional workers would help advance their business opportunities.[120]

Kennedy's executive order did increase Black employment somewhat, but much more significant gains resulted from the Equal Employment Opportunity Commission and legislation developed under President Lyndon Johnson.[121] By 1966, towns like Greenville, South Carolina, had doubled their Black male employee population and began to hire Black women as well.[122] By 1970 in South Carolina, Black people made up 20 percent of textile employees.[123] This is just one example of a strategy that

---

[118] Albert Muzquiz, "Black America's Hard Fought Integration of Southern Textile Mills," Heddels, June 24, 2020, https://www.heddels.com/2020/06/segregation-in-southern-textile-mills/.

[119] Judy Bainbridge, "How Black Workers Changed the Textile Industry in South Carolina," *Greenville News*, October 29, 2018, https://www.greenvilleonline.com/story/news/2018/10/29/how-black-workers-changed-textile-industry-south-carolina/1798644002/.

[120] Bainbridge, "How Black Workers Changed the Textile Industry in South Carolina."

[121] Bainbridge, "How Black Workers Changed the Textile Industry in South Carolina."

[122] Bainbridge, "How Black Workers Changed the Textile Industry in South Carolina."

[123] Bainbridge, "How Black Workers Changed the Textile Industry in South Carolina."

addressed a real-world economic need to the mutual benefit of textile owners, workers, and the U.S. government (which was in need of the goods
produced). However, much of this progress was eventually stalled by
automation, cheaper imports, and the push toward globalization into the
1980s and 1990s—a period often referred to as "deindustrialization."[124]

The deindustrialization of significant American industries led to
massive economic impacts on rural and urban communities.[125] What had
begun around the time of the Civil War as an increase in jobs and commerce through advancements such as railroad development and agricultural mechanisms became huge opportunities for the labor force and the
associated economic development for the surrounding communities.[126]
Other than during the Great Depression, this increase continued through
the 1950s and led to population and city growth around the country,
including places like New York, Philadelphia, St. Louis, Chicago, and
Detroit.[127] This era of technical innovations and mass production remained strong into the 1970s, at which time international competitors
like Japan, China, and Germany began to take over much of the market
share.[128] This competition had a massive impact on urban areas in particular, leading to job losses, loss of tax bases, reduced government services,
and in some cases the eventual economic collapse of cities themselves.[129]
Within the social fabric of these communities, these circumstances led
to mass unemployment, poverty, family strife, violence, and criminal

---

[124] Bainbridge, "How Black Workers Changed the Textile Industry in South
       Carolina."
[125] "Deindustrialization and the American City," The Consilience Project,
       February 22, 2021, https://consilienceproject.org/deindustrialization-and-the-
       american-city/.
[126] "Deindustrialization and the American City."
[127] "Deindustrialization and the American City."
[128] "Deindustrialization and the American City."
[129] "Deindustrialization and the American City."

activity.[130] They also led to racial tension, as many of these communities were home to Black families who had left the South to come to the North for the opportunities that industrialization brought with it—a period termed the "Great Migration."[131]

Infighting and riots resulted, such as in Detroit in 1967, which caused many people to leave urban areas—often referred to as "White Flight."[132] While some of the big cities lost up to 40 percent of their population during deindustrialization, communities within the Rust Belt (such as Youngstown, Ohio) experienced seemingly insurmountable damage— with losses of $400 million in personal income and forty thousand manufacturing jobs, and the closure of four hundred businesses in just a few years.[133] This wave of closures also hit places like Gary, Indiana hard, where at one point almost 20 percent of residents lived in poverty due to the closure of its major factory.[134] Historical circumstances like these have led to limited economic and employment advancement for many of the underserved today, as these people may have been placed in situations with few educational opportunities or job-skills programs and now must simply remain stuck in an unforgiving system.

And even in the face of this, what has been the federal government's policy response? Under President Bill Clinton, America turned its attention to globalization—outsourcing technology and jobs to the rest of the world.[135] While luckily, some of the national economic impact was mitigated by the beginnings of the internet/dot-com boom in the 1990s,

---

[130] "Deindustrialization and the American City."
[131] "Deindustrialization and the American City."
[132] "Deindustrialization and the American City."
[133] "Deindustrialization and the American City."
[134] "Deindustrialization and the American City."
[135] President Clinton stated, *"So the great question before us is not whether globalization will proceed, but how? And what is our responsibility in the developed world to try to shape this process so that it lifts people in all nations."* Brian Williams, "Clinton Sees Globalization As Key Issue," Institute for

the globalization effort exacerbated job losses within the United States, as corporations were able to pay foreign workers pennies on the dollar for what had been American jobs—many of which had traditionally been held by Black people and other minorities. Further, implemented under the likely well-intentioned theory of globalization that sharing certain technologies would lift up the poor populations of other countries, innovations in those same technologies and industries ultimately resulted in American reliance on foreign countries for many basic products—impacting the job market and supply chains as recently as 2022. Consistent during globalization, and for many decades earlier, have been social programs put in place to purportedly lift poor people out of a lower economic class; however, these programs have played a key role in establishing dependency and a lack of advancement for many members of underserved communities.

In modern America, the Democratic party has based significant portions of its political philosophy on the fact that so-called social safety-net programs not only must exist but must exist in seeming perpetuity. At first glance, this sounds like the basis for a utopian society where everyone's needs are met simply by living in America; however, this philosophy has created not only dependence but the unrealistic expectation that these benefits will always be there. As such, there is no incentive to take any other action than to apply for federal government benefits—rinse and repeat. This approach not only fosters a blind dependence on the programs, it all but ensures that many people will never achieve any economic viability beyond the minimum standards set by the federal government. Ironically, by providing financial and other resources with no real timetable or incentive to advance beyond them, these programs stifle a traditional economic market that not only includes supply and demand, but still assumes that rational participants will act in a manner to achieve

Agriculture and Trade Policy, December 14, 2000, https://www.iatp.org/news/clinton-sees-globalization-as-key-issue.

their greatest benefit. The greatest economic benefit here is a false choice, as these individuals have been presented not with the limitless opportunity of America's capitalist economy but with the ceiling of whatever federal government benefits they can cobble together. In fact, they are given the unwarranted dilemma of comparing the dollar value of a job to the dollar value of a program for which they may continue to qualify if they do not seek out that job. Further, given the many decades of this approach, an intergenerational impact has developed, and many people view government programs as their only opportunities for survival.

And here is where it gets worse. This dependency has become institutionalized, not just for those who have inadvertently bound themselves to these programs but for liberal politicians who count on these individuals as a voting base. There is a political reality that purportedly *fighting* for these people is simply a way to continue the cycle of this market failure and maintain time in office. This undermines the concept of limited government and actually creates a *limiting* government that does not provide a social safety net for those who actually need it, but rather only for those who either want it or have been led to believe that it is all they can achieve.

Conservative thinkers have warned of these possibilities for centuries. Take, for example, renowned 1700s conservative Edmund Burke, who famously wrote about the tyranny of English King George III, as well as the French Revolution. He noted that "it is a general popular error to suppose the loudest complainers for the public to be the most anxious for its welfare," demonstrating that those who say they are fighting for the underserved in the context of economic programs may not in fact have the welfare of the general public in mind.[136] Burke went on to state that "hypocrisy can afford to be magnificent in its promises, for never

---

[136] "Thoughts on the Business of Life: Edmund Burke Quotes," *Forbes*, https://www.forbes.com/quotes/author/edmund-burke/.

intending to go beyond promise, it costs nothing."[137] This clearly shows that liberal politicians who continually promise more and more government involvement are not bound by any real outcome—as continual election to office is their desired goal. While one could make the argument that their efforts yield mutual benefit—the politician and the constituent get access to votes and funds, respectively—such an argument does not address the fact that this approach forces the constituents to settle and limits their ability to achieve their highest economic potential.

Conservative critics of the liberal politicians' approach may be deemed heartless as some may say they are not accounting for the truly needy. Nothing could be further from the truth, as conservative ideals include taking steps to provide for those who truly need it. In fact, one individual who espoused taking these steps was Alexander Hamilton, who is known today more for the theatrical version of his life than for his conservative bona fides. He is one of the authors of the "Federalist Papers," was the first secretary of the Department of Treasury, and advocated for developing the country's credit as a means to promote trade to benefit America, believing in the positive downstream effects of commerce on sustainable economic conditions, which would ultimately support peaceable conditions for the citizenry. Among his many notable statements, Hamilton is famous for writing that "happy it is when the interest which the government has in the preservation of its own power, coincides with a proper distribution of the public burthens [*sic*], and tends to guard the least wealthy part of the community from oppression!"[138] While Hamilton's belief in a strong central government had significant economic roots, this quote identifies his recognition that a nation must account for those who need economic support. This is a critical recognition, as his conservative

---

[137] "Thoughts on the Business of Life: Edmund Burke Quotes."
[138] Alexander Hamilton, Federalist Papers No. 36, https://avalon.law.yale.edu/18th_century/fed36.asp.

pedigree is without question and identifies clear support for underserved communities.

If you accept the premise that in part, reliance on government programs has led to market failure, but that it is also a tenet of conservatism to care for the underserved, what is the appropriate framework to achieve that end? Conservative Frenchman Alexis de Tocqueville opined that the systems of state welfare for the poor and unemployed could ultimately present the unintended consequence of dependence by the underserved. He stated that "democracy seeks equality in liberty, socialism seeks equality in restraint and servitude."[139] He more fully explained this position, showing that a socialist government approach "does not tyrannise but it compresses, enervates, extinguishes, and stupefies a people, till each nation is reduced to nothing better than a flock of timid and industrious animals, of which the government is the shepherd."[140]

As a political observer of the impacts of the revolutions in France and America, Tocqueville serves as a thoughtful witness to social circumstances that can escalate into drastic and potentially violent actions. His conclusion suggests that ongoing government dependence can have disastrous consequences and undermine the principles of traditional democracy. His thinking set forth above largely speaks for itself, highlighting that the freedoms of democracy exist to support the contributions of the individual, and thereby help individuals thrive. His words are some of the most illustrative when it comes to underserved communities. They clearly underscore the idea that prolonged programs meant to satiate only the most basic needs can become all that people believe they are entitled

---

[139] Mitch Pearlstein, "Alexis de Tocqueville on Sanders and Socialism," American Experiment, February 13, 2019, https://www.americanexperiment.org/alexis-de-tocqueville-on-sanders-and-socialism/.

[140] Mark J. Perry, "Quotation of the Day: Alexis De Tocqueville on Despotism," American Enterprise Institute, July 19, 2013, https://www.aei.org/carpe-diem/quotation-of-the-day-alexis-de-tocqueville-on-despotism/.

to, and that they stifle not only ambition but opportunity, thereby undermining the benefit of that individual's potential contributions to the nation.

Tocqueville's positions are often echoed by other conservatives, including Nobel Prize–winning economist Friedrich Hayek, who famously wrote in his book *The Road to Serfdom*, "There is all the difference in the world between treating people equally and attempting to make them equal." He further illustrated the true economic framework for his position when he wrote in *A Free-Market Monetary System and The Pretense of Knowledge*:

> *The public at large have learned to understand...that government has the power in the short run by increasing the quantity of money rapidly to relieve all kinds of economic evils, especially to reduce unemployment. Unfortunately this is true so far as the short run is concerned. The fact is, that such expansions of the quantity of money which seems to have a short run beneficial effect, become in the long run the cause of a much greater unemployment. But what politician can possibly care about long run effects if in the short run he buys support?*

As an economist, Hayek saw the free market as the perfect vehicle for business—promoting opportunity and competition—while his theories recognize that people may need to be treated differently for them to achieve the same result.[141] That said, he noted that treating people differently can perpetuate a system by which one class eventually becomes dependent on a certain political class.[142] His work underscores the unde-

---

[141] Arthur Kaledin, "Class: Between Two Worlds," in *Tocqueville and His America* (Yale University Press, August 2011).

[142] Kaledin, "Class: Between Two Worlds."

niable narrative that perpetual dependency limits economic freedom and hurts the class it purports to assist.

Another famed economist who has already been referenced is Milton Friedman, a Nobel Prize winner who taught at the University of Chicago. He advised Presidents Nixon and Reagan, and he supported a variety of public and social policies, including school vouchers and a balanced-budget amendment.[143] Friedman's contributions to economic theory are numerous, and his writings certainly support the ongoing conservative position that privilege cannot be perpetual in a functional free market, and that ambition and competition are critical to allow for economic opportunity and advancement.[144] He articulated his position in this way: "Freedom means diversity but also mobility. It preserves the opportunity for today's disadvantaged to become tomorrow's privileged and, in the process, enables almost everyone, from top to bottom, to enjoy a fuller and richer life."[145]

All of the philosophical, economic, and theoretical concepts described above have had many vessels over the past fifty years, but one politician in particular married them in a way that embraces both the head and

---

[143] "Milton Friedman: Biographical," Nobel Prize Outreach, https://www.nobel-prize.org/prizes/economic-sciences/1976/friedman/biographical/.

[144] *"On the other hand, a society that puts freedom first will, as a happy by-product, end up with both greater freedom and greater equality. Though a by-product of freedom, greater equality is not an accident. A free society releases the energies and abilities of people to pursue their own objectives. It prevents some people from arbitrarily suppressing others. It does not prevent some people from achieving positions of privilege, but so long as freedom is maintained, it prevents those positions of privilege from becoming institutionalized; they are subject to continued attack by other able, ambitious people. Freedom means diversity but also mobility. It preserves the opportunity for today's disadvantaged to become tomorrow's privileged and, in the process, enables almost everyone, from top to bottom, to enjoy a fuller and richer life."* Milton Friedman, "What Does 'God Created Equal' Mean?" Hoover Institute, March 8, 2018, https://www.hoover.org/research/what-does-created-equal-mean.

[145] Friedman, "What Does 'God Created Equal' Mean?"

the heart. Jack Kemp, a professional football player, congressman, secretary of the Department of Housing and Urban and Development, and Republican vice presidential candidate, amplified the Republican party's role in advancing underserved communities. A passionate conservative on economic policies, he also supported strong civil rights legislation and economic policies that sought to advance underserved communities. His practical application of the theories discussed herein began to generate formulas for implementation of these ideals, as in: "conservatives define compassion not by the number of people who receive some kind of government aid but rather by the number of people who no longer need it."[146] He saw that for government aid to become unnecessary, not only must identifiable progress be made, but the impact of that progress must be captured in true economic terms—such as in the number of jobs held and homes ownership—stating, "When people lack jobs, opportunity, and ownership of property they have little or no stake in their communities."[147]

Finally, we turn to Stanford University professor Thomas Sowell, an influential Black economist and modern thought leader on the issues facing underserved communities. His academic positions are buttressed with immutable evidence, but more importantly, his solutions are blunt and actionable—particularly for the modern Black community—as exemplified by statements such as, "When you want to help people, you tell them the truth. When you want to help yourself, you tell them what they want to hear. People with careers as ethnic leaders usually tell their followers what they want to hear."[148] Sowell's criticism underscores the concern that many purported modern leaders are self-interested. Whether

[146] "Jack Kemp Quotes," AZ Quotes, https://www.azquotes.com/author/7876-Jack_Kemp.

[147] "Jack Kemp Quotes."

[148] "Thomas Sowell Quotes," Quotefancy, https://quotefancy.com/quote/2944820/Thomas-Sowell-When-you-want-to-help-people-you-tell-them-the-truth-When-you-want-to-help.

it is for fear of losing elected office or impact on fundraising dollars for their organizations, speaking truthfully on what it will take to change the current cycle and correct the associated market failure may not be comfortable. Sowell states that "drawing up policy blueprints is a task for which there has never been a shortage of eager candidates. We can only hope that those policies will be based on hard facts about the real world, rather than on rhetoric or preconceptions."[149] Drawing up this type of foundational policy blueprint is what this book seeks to achieve.

The above snapshot of conservative leaders does more than demonstrate their commitment to free markets; it lays the foundation for the importance of economic mobility for underserved communities. Burke shows us that actions and strategy supplant boisterous verbiage and short-sighted empty promises, while Hamilton supports traditional rights and opportunities for the underserved. Tocqueville abhors the use of social programs that create generations of dependent communities, and with this in mind, economists such as Hayek see a world where intentional and actionable steps may need to be taken to achieve this vision to enhance these opportunities. Friedman's position further bolsters the concept that privilege cannot be perpetual in a free market; and all of this is brought together by politicians like Jack Kemp, who hold dear the idea that compassion rests in taking the necessary actions to lift people out of the need for government programs, and observers like Sowell, who demand an honest conversation about how that can occur.

---

[149] "Thomas Sowell Quotes," Goodreads, https://www.goodreads.com/author/quotes/2056.Thomas_Sowell?page=21.

CHAPTER **FOUR**

Education, Workforce, and the Trump Administration's Response: The Pledge to America's Workers and HBCU Funding

In an 1861 address to Congress, Abraham Lincoln explained that his purpose as President of the United States was "to elevate the condition of man."[150] A critical component of that elevation was education. Lincoln grew up in the prairie country of the Midwest, educating himself in a land with limited infrastructure to support the agrarian economy—and as such, those agricultural jobs most often were the only work available. Under Lincoln's leadership, the Morrill Land Grant College Act of 1862 was passed, and the profits from lands obtained by the federal government became something of an equalizer, as the act initiated the creation of land grant colleges throughout the country—which became the beginnings of the state university system.[151] Whereas the existing Ivy

---

[150] "The Way That Lincoln Financed the Civil War Led to Transcontinental Railroads, Public Colleges, and the Homestead Act and Income Tax," *History Unplugged Podcast.*

[151] *Reconstruction: America After the Civil War.*

League schools were often associated more with social status and often impractical academia, these schools would teach students pragmatic skills that could advance their opportunities across geographies and industries. While it should be noted that this educational achievement was made possible in part at the expense of the indigenous peoples from whom the lands were confiscated, the Morrill Act is also credited with opening up educational pathways in subjects such as agriculture, mechanical arts, and engineering in order to support business development.[152]

It is also noteworthy that the proposal and implementation of this legislation were undertaken during the midst of the Civil War, stressing the importance of the educational need and providing for economic opportunity for people to leave crowded cities, to go west and settle—contributing to the growth of America.[153] Further, in line with the Union's ultimate objectives, these newly educated individuals would go make their own occupational opportunities and would not necessarily seek to be reliant upon or in competition with slaves—thereby advancing abolition from an economic perspective.[154] The act also led to the beginnings of academic research and development funding, much of which has created significant societal impact across countless disciplines.[155] And of course public-private partnerships between the federal government, foundations, and universities remain strong today across many industries, including in areas of small business engagement. For example, the

---

[152] Colleen LaRose, "Workforce Development in America: A Brief History," LinkedIn article, October 15, 2014, https://www.linkedin.com/pulse/20141015154244-57121104-workforce-development-in-america-a-brief-history/.

[153] "The Way that Lincoln Financed the Civil War Led to Transcontinental Railroads, Public Colleges, the Homestead Act and Income Tax."

[154] "The Way that Lincoln Financed the Civil War Led to Transcontinental Railroads, Public Colleges, the Homestead Act and Income Tax."

[155] "The Way that Lincoln Financed the Civil War Led to Transcontinental Railroads, Public Colleges, the Homestead Act and Income Tax."

U.S. Small Business Administration (SBA) oversees the Small Business Innovation Research (SBIR) and Small Business Technology Transfer (STTR) programs, which have launched numerous small businesses, created countless jobs, and led to the creation of critical commercial and consumer products for America and the world. SBIR and STTR opportunities begin as grants that can turn into federal government contracts; and these contracts provide critical support to areas such as national security, agriculture, transportation, and space exploration, as well as give entrepreneurs a pathway to commercialize their hard work, talent, and ingenuity through private sector companies, which in turn can generate significant economic and employment opportunities.

The societal impact of the Morrill Act remains an important benchmark for higher education in this country, and establishes a direct connection between educational opportunities, research grants, and workforce development efforts throughout underserved communities. The term "workforce development" can mean many things to many people. The Federal Reserve defines it as "a relatively wide range of activities, policies and programs employed by geographies to create, sustain and retain a viable workforce that can support current and future business and industry."[156] Prior to the Civil War, higher education was more focused on philosophy and humanistic reasoning and did not necessarily embrace vocational techniques.[157] As such, the Morrill Act provided educational opportunities *and* stressed the importance of encouraging access to mechanical training for middle-class professions. And this kind of training of course provides a workforce that helps to generate revenues that support capital investment, which can lead to innovations and overall mutual benefit for all parties involved.

However, in 1929, with the Wall Street crash and the subsequent Great Depression, most of these mutually beneficial opportunities disappeared

---

[156] LaRose, "Workforce Development in America: A Brief History."
[157] LaRose, "Workforce Development in America: A Brief History."

overnight, which set the stage for President Franklin Roosevelt's New Deal—a panoply of programs and agencies to address lost employment opportunities, a devastated economy, and certain institutional government reforms.[158] One of the agencies created was the Works Progress Administration (WPA), renamed the Work Projects Administration in 1939.[159] The WPA's purpose was to oversee the development, implementation, and construction of public infrastructure, such as buildings and roads.[160] It was initially appropriated almost $5 billion, and went on to spend approximately $13.5 billion.[161] Ultimately employing almost eight million people, the WPA sought to provide a job to at least one member of every family in which the main breadwinner was unemployed, where the end goal was to remove public assistance per se and advance the concept of work relief in order to reinforce skills, work ethic, and the dignity of a job.[162] Due to low unemployment during World War II, the WPA was ended in 1943.[163] Something of a companion program was also established under the Wagner-Peyser Act of 1933, which established a system that sought to match people with employment, and notably provided states with federal grants to achieve this goal.[164]

As a kind of successor to Roosevelt in this space, President Lyndon Johnson sought to implement the Great Society during his tenure, along with his War on Poverty. The legislative portfolio included numerous programs and had workforce development components, such as the programs associated with the Economic Opportunity Act of 1964 (EOA).[165] The EOA established government programs that became well-known

---

[158] LaRose, "Workforce Development in America: A Brief History."
[159] LaRose, "Workforce Development in America: A Brief History."
[160] LaRose, "Workforce Development in America: A Brief History."
[161] LaRose, "Workforce Development in America: A Brief History."
[162] LaRose, "Workforce Development in America: A Brief History.".
[163] LaRose, "Workforce Development in America: A Brief History."
[164] LaRose, "Workforce Development in America: A Brief History."
[165] LaRose, "Workforce Development in America: A Brief History."

and components of which still continue to this day—such as Vista, Head Start, and the Job Corps, which concentrate on employment and training efforts in distressed areas.[166] The Manpower Development and Training Act of 1962 (MDTA) was also passed under President Lyndon Johnson. This legislation was not necessarily focused on poverty or the underserved, but rather sought to provide transitional programming for workers who had lost their employment due to technological advances.[167]

The MDTA was replaced by the Comprehensive Employment Training Act of 1973, which created a decentralized federal block grant program.[168] Local communities had much of the control, as funds were distributed to states by the federal government and then handed down to targeted municipalities.[169] In the wake of allegations of mismanagement and corruption by local partners, the regulations became overburdensome, and the 1973 act was ultimately replaced by the Job Training Partnership Act of 1982.[170] This legislation focused on low-income populations, removed public sector employment components, and relied more on local governance councils.[171] Under the direction of its Employment and Training Administration, the Department of Labor also engaged in this community-based approach using state and local grants for workforce development from the National Employment Service, which had been created as part of the Wagner-Peyser Act.[172]

In 1998, under President Bill Clinton, Congress passed the Workforce Investment Act (WIA), which established a division in the Department of Labor that sought to provide comprehensive services in a manner that

166 LaRose, "Workforce Development in America: A Brief History."
167 LaRose, "Workforce Development in America: A Brief History."
168 LaRose, "Workforce Development in America: A Brief History."
169 LaRose, "Workforce Development in America: A Brief History."
170 LaRose, "Workforce Development in America: A Brief History."
171 LaRose, "Workforce Development in America: A Brief History."
172 LaRose, "Workforce Development in America: A Brief History."

accounted for local economic development plans, and engaged directly with potential employers.[173] The national locations within this network are referred to as American Job Centers, each of which provides vouchers for eligible employment training. The WIA was reauthorized in 2014 with bipartisan support with certain improvements, such as unified workforce plans and standardized performance metrics.[174] Under its new name, the Workforce Innovation and Opportunity Act (WIOA), it included specific programs to support impacted workers, all of which permit users to work directly with local case managers on issues such as literacy, rehabilitation, guidance counseling, and of course job placement. [175]

Notwithstanding all of the legislation over those several decades to promote workforce development through both education and opportunity, the skills gap remains dangerously apparent in underserved communities— particularly in rural areas. While many may assume that farm bills and associated subsidies address large swaths of these communities, they would be mistaken to believe that the totality of their needs are being addressed.[176] Recognition of the skills gap goes back to Presidents Theodore and Franklin Roosevelt. In 1909, Teddy established the Country Life Commission to examine how rural America was growing beyond farming, and that commission recommended establishing a federal agency that would focus just on rural areas.[177] And, as previously discussed, while FDR's WPA provided

---

[173] LaRose, "Workforce Development in America: A Brief History."

[174] Kevin Bauman and Cody Christensen, "Improving Skills Through America's Workforce Development System," American Enterprise Institute I, September 11, 2018, https://www.aei.org/research-products/report/improving-skills-through-americas-workforce-development-system/.

[175] Bauman and Christensen, "Improving Skills Through America's Workforce Development System."

[176] David Freshwater, "The Elusive Promise of U.S. Rural Policy," in *Investing in Rural Property*, eds. Andrew Dumont and Daniel Paul Davis (Federal Reserve Bank of St. Louis, 2021), 31.

[177] Freshwater, "The Elusive Promise of U.S. Rural Policy," 32.

public works opportunities to rural areas, unfortunately much of those efforts benefited the larger farms and producers.[178]

Eventually, in the 1940s, rural electrification came about, and the Department of Agriculture spearheaded more infrastructure programs.[179] To date, rural areas still struggle with a unified approach to advancement, and in many places, the lack of such a policy has led to a very limited middle class, high-poverty counties, and low levels of education.[180] In fact, approximately 86 percent of persistent-poverty counties have unemployment rates well in excess of the national average, and opioid addiction in these areas seems to have outpaced most other parts of the country.[181]

These disparities between rural and urban opportunities and the associated poverty rate in rural areas was captured in President Lyndon Johnson's 1967 report *The People Left Behind*, which identified the rural rate of poverty as being 25 percent—approximately double the urban rate.[182] More than fifty years later, the wages for many rural residents have not increased substantially, and in 2016, only half of low-skilled workers in rural areas were working, compared with 65 percent of their counterparts in urban areas.[183] In addition, the difference in the rates of college attendance for rural versus urban workers has grown from 5 to 20 percent over the past fifty years, and unemployment numbers have consistently been high for Black people in rural areas.[184] The circumstances of this concentrated poverty contribute

---

[178] David Danbom, *Born in Country: A History of Rural America* (Johns Hopkins University Press, 2017), 205.

[179] Freshwater, "The Elusive Promise of U.S. Rural Policy," 37.

[180] Daniel Lichter and Kenneth Johnson, "Marginalization of Rural Communities in the U.S.," in *Investing in Rural Prosperity*, 52.

[181] Lichter and Johnson, "Marginalization of Rural Communities in the U.S.," 58.

[182] "Many Rural Americans Are Still 'Left Behind,'" Institute for Research on Poverty, January 2020, https://www.irp.wisc.edu/resource/many-rural-americans-are-still-left-behind/.

[183] "Many Rural Americans Are Still 'Left Behind.'"

[184] "Many Rural Americans Are Still 'Left Behind.'"

to poor health, substandard housing, limited education, and higher crime rates.[185] But, as has been discussed, the deindustrialization period of the 1980s and 1990s had a devastating effect on these communities and ultimately removed many of the opportunities that once existed. In more recent times, the rural areas of the southern United States have had a poverty rate just under 20 percent, and a key driver has been deindustrialization.

Fast-forward to today, when there is an emerging employment skills gap in the labor market.[186] This is significantly found in middle-skill jobs, which are typically jobs that do not require a four-year college degree. Studies have shown that while these jobs account for over half of the U.S. labor market, less than half of the labor force has received sufficient training to perform these roles—leading to depressed earnings and reductions in productivity.[187] While as many as 35 percent of jobs in the U.S. are at risk of being automated within the next twenty years according to some estimates, many of these middle-skill jobs will continue to be in high demand for the foreseeable future—including components of industries that cannot be easily automated, such as health care. [188] Private employers are also providing training for certain roles, with more than two-thirds of U.S. companies providing some form of a workforce training curriculum—frequently leading to reduced worker turnover, greater productivity, and higher wages.[189] However, this training is often reserved for those already employed at these firms. It is somewhat uncommon to find apprenticeship-style opportunities

---

[185] "Rural Poverty & Well-Being," Economic Research Service, November 29, 2022, https://www.ers.usda.gov/topics/rural-economy-population/rural-poverty-well-being/.

[186] Bauman and Christensen, "Improving Skills Through America's Workforce Development System."

[187] Bauman and Christensen, "Improving Skills Through America's Workforce Development System."

[188] Bauman and Christensen, "Improving Skills Through America's Workforce Development System."

[189] Bauman and Christensen, "Improving Skills Through America's Workforce Development System."

at these companies to leverage the available training, and as such, this kind of training has limited impact on the chronically unemployed.[190]

Recognizing all of this, President Trump signed an executive order in 2018 that focused on his Pledge to America's Workers.[191] The rationale for this initiative was the fact that the country was facing a skills crisis, and at the time there were almost seven million unfilled American jobs. Further, with a rapidly developing economy that prioritizes technological solutions, automation alternatives, and artificial intelligence, there is an immediate need to prepare American workers and connect them to the future. Further, in order to ensure that this training would be relevant at the time of the order and in the future, the administration had to include a lifelong learning component for workers, so they could keep up with technological innovation and the associated developing job opportunities. In order to accomplish this, the administration needed to partner with the private sector to ensure that workers would be well positioned to be trained for and connected to the open positions. As such, "private employers, educational institutions, labor unions, other non-profit organizations, and State, territorial, tribal, and local governments" were incorporated into the plan and were teamed up with relevant cabinet secretaries, including the leaders of the Departments of Commerce and Treasury, as well as with agencies such as the SBA, Veterans Affairs, the White House's Office of Management and Budget, the National Economic Council, and the Council of Economic Advisors.[192] The key deliverables of President Trump's directive, as led by Senior Advisor Ivanka Trump and the secretaries of the Departments of

---

[190] Bauman and Christensen, "Improving Skills Through America's Workforce Development System."

[191] "Executive Order Establishing the President's National Council for the American Worker," July 19, 2018, https://trumpwhitehouse.archives.gov/presidential-actions/executive-order-establishing-presidents-national-council-american-worker/.

[192] "Executive Order Establishing the President's National Council for the American Worker."

Commerce and Labor, included coordination, cooperation, and information sharing among all of these groups through a national campaign that would include training, retraining, credentialing, apprenticeships, online resources, and ongoing public-private partnerships.

To put this period in context, the U.S. economy became incredibly strong in 2017 into 2019. In fact, businesses could not hire fast enough. Unemployment was historically low across all demographic groups, and various agencies—including the SBA—held events and conferences to invigorate hiring opportunities for disadvantaged groups. To coordinate opportunities for these Americans, the leadership of this effort spearheaded this national initiative to work directly with corporate CEOs to hire, as well as to provide training and a chance for workers to be reskilled and receive apprenticeships and continuing education. All of these efforts resulted in the identification of over sixteen million employment opportunities.[193] With notable companies and key trade association partners—such as IBM, Apple, the U.S. Chamber of Commerce, and the National Association of Manufacturing—the program made significant strides quickly. Plenty of examples were noted across the country, and novel methods of engagement accelerated quickly in order to advance such a unique effort. One example of engagement was a rural tour by SBA Administrator Linda McMahon and Department of Agriculture Secretary Sonny Perdue to help empower farmers and start-ups located in rural areas with access to capital. Key SBA initiatives also included McMahon's Ascent technology platform, which sought to help women entrepreneurs in the various stages of their business growth.[194] A successful businesswomen

[193] "Pledge to America's Workers," https://trumpwhitehouse.archives.gov/pledge-to-americas-workers/#:~:text=The%20Pledge%20to%20America's%20Workers,-As%20part%20of&text=Since%20President%20Trump%20signed%20the,over%20the%20next%20five%20years.

[194] "Trump Administration Invests $871 Million in Rural Community Facilities in 43 States and Guam: New Schools, Health Clinics and Public Safety Facilities Will Benefit 3.5 Million People," USDA

herself, McMahon knew firsthand that the most difficult thing for these entrepreneurs to do was to scale their businesses, so working closely with the Department of Labor and Ivanka Trump, she championed an SBA effort to establish the multimedia Ascent platform. This novel technology was and still is able be accessed virtually, and continues to serve as an important resource for a growing ecosystem of women entrepreneurs.[195]

As a cabinet member who succeeded McMahon, coauthor Chris Pilkerton had the unique opportunity to be a part of the Pledge to America's Workers program on a trip to Calumet, a small community in Michigan's Upper Peninsula.[196] He began that trip with a tour of a coffee shop called 5th and Elm, which had been devastated by a significant flood and had been the recipient of an SBA-backed small business disaster loan. After that meeting, he went on to the main part of his visit, which was a tour of Calumet Electronics. Once the mining capital of Michigan, producing half of the copper in the United States in the 1870s, the town of Calumet had been hit hard in the decades up through the Great Depression, as mining ceased and the community was impacted accordingly. But over the years, one of its strongest businesses—Calumet Electronics, a circuit board manufacturing and engineering firm—had become part of President Trump's pledge. As such, it committed to educating and reskilling workers alongside its three hundred employees, making its products with American-made parts. Chris' tour of the facility included meeting many of the company's employees and their families, and he was incredibly moved not just by their commitment to reskilling but by their obvious pride in the community. Chris visited Michigan

---

Press, October 28, 2020, https://www.usda.gov/media/press-releases/2020/10/28/trump-administration-invests-871-million-rural-community-facilities.

[195] U.S. Small Business Administration, Ascent platform, https://ascent.sba.gov/.

[196] Garrett Neese, "Cabinet Member Visits Calumet Electronics," *The Daily News*, July 25, 2019, https://www.ironmountaindailynews.com/news/2019/07/cabinet-member-visits-calumet-electronics/.

Technological University as well, in order to learn more about its engagement with the local high school STEM programs and its training efforts in the areas of robotics, energy, electronics, and space, among others.

Among the many students and employees that Chris met at Calumet Electronics was Michigan Tech alum Audra Thurston.[197] A 2018 graduate with a degree in chemical engineering, Thurston landed an internship at the electronics company, which led to a career in circuit board development, as well as a trip to the White House in 2019 to meet with President Trump, Vice President Pence, and Ivanka Trump at an event acknowledging the many companies that were participating in the Pledge program.[198] While many people would understandably be a bit overwhelmed in the White House meeting those people, Chris recalls the pride with which Thurston represented Calumet, as well as the promise that she represented for that community.

While this is simply one story of the many, many commitments associated with this program, it serves as a firsthand account of the serious work done by countless officials in the Trump administration to advance efforts for workers and small businesses. And these efforts for workers of course were a critical component of a plan to improve the economic opportunities of underserved communities. But the administration did not stop there. Under the leadership of U.S. Trade Representative Robert Lighthizer, the administration engaged in an effort to replace the North American Free Trade Agreement (NAFTA) with the United States-Mexico-Canada Agreement (USMCA)—with a particular

---

[197] Mark Wilcox, "A Perfect Example: Alumna's Story Told at Round Table," *Michigan Tech News*, July 25, 2019, https://www.mtu.edu/news/2019/07/a-perfect-example-alumnas-story-told-at-round-table.html.

[198] "Calumet Electronics Engineer to Meet with President Trump Thursday," Upper Michigan Source, July 24, 2019, https://www.uppermichiganssource.com/content/news/Calumet-Electronics-engineer-to-meet-with-President-Trump-Thursday-513164031.html.

focus on creating a level playing field for North American workers, farmers, ranchers, and businesses. While there will be books written on the USMCA's content and impact, one of the most novel components of the agreement is that, under the leadership of Administrator McMahon, it was the first international trade agreement to have an entire chapter focused on small businesses. This is so important, as so many of these businesses are the economic drivers of underinvested communities, and small businesses make up 96 percent of all U.S. exporters, ultimately accounting for a total of 26 percent of all U.S. exports.[199] This policy approach has helped create more jobs in underserved communities, which of course has led to enhanced economic development opportunities.

While serving in SBA leadership, Chris also had the opportunity to travel significantly to talk about some of this work, including a tour of colleges in North Carolina, such as Shaw University and Saint Augustine's University, both HBCUs. Spending time at these schools and meeting some of their leaders made Chris proud of the work that the Trump administration was doing to support these important institutions that hold such a unique role in our country's history. The first HBCU, called the African Institute, was established in Pennsylvania by Richard Humphreys in 1837, and since has been renamed Cheyney University of Pennsylvania.[200] Back then, its curriculum focused on skills to provide for gainful employment—such as math, reading, and writing, as well as the industrial arts. Within the next two decades, three more HBCUs were founded in Washington, D.C., Pennsylvania, and Ohio—Miner Normal School, Lincoln University, and Wilberforce University, respectively. Wilberforce was the first university to be operated by Black people.[201]

---

[199] "Small Business Administration Trade and Export Promotion Programs," Congressional Research Service, May 24, 2022, https://sgp.fas.org/crs/misc/R43155.pdf.

[200] "History of Cheyney University," Cheyney University, https://cheyney.edu/for-parents/history-traditions/.

[201] Thurgood Marshall College Fund, https://www.tmcf.org/.

Before the beginning of the Civil War, approximately 90 percent of the Black slave population was illiterate, as were half of the five hundred thousand free Black people.[202] In 1861, as the Civil War began, the Morrill Land Grant College Act, assisted by private sector support, served as a catalyst to grow the number of Black schools.[203] HBCUs provided high school educations as well at this time, and by the time a second Morrill Act was passed in 1890, and the "separate but equal" Supreme Court decision in *Plessy v. Ferguson* was handed down, most HBCUs focused their teaching on a postsecondary curriculum.[204] Within forty-five years from the end of slavery, there were eight hundred Black schools, and by 1943, there were nearly two hundred and fifty HBCUs.[205] Teaching students received grants from philanthropists to attend Northern schools like Columbia University to enhance their credentials, and additional feeder program schools were established by state departments of education. By 1955, Howard University became the first HBCU to offer a doctorate degree, and many of the leaders of the civil rights movement of the 1960s were proud alums of Howard and other Black universities.[206] Today, about 89 percent of HBCUs can be found in the South—Alabama, North Carolina, and Louisiana have the most—and these universities have student enrollments ranging from three hundred to over eleven thousand students.[207] While Presidents Richard Nixon, Gerald Ford, and Jimmy Carter all increased federal support for the HBCU community, these schools have faced innumerable challenges over the years.[208] Still,

---

[202] *Reconstruction: America After the Civil War.*

[203] B. Lovett, *History of Historically Black Colleges and Universities: A Narrative History 1837-2009* (Mercer University Press, 2015), preface.

[204] See www.blackpast.org.

[205] Lovett, *History of Historically Black Colleges and Universities*, preface.

[206] Lovett, *History of Historically Black Colleges and Universities*, preface.

[207] Thurgood Marshall College Fund.

[208] Lovett, *History of Historically Black Colleges and Universities*, preface.

it is of note that today two-thirds of Black doctors, federal judges, and military leaders attended an HBCU.[209]

Coauthor Ja'Ron Smith recalls when he first heard about HBCUs as a young man. It never occurred to him as a kid that a popular television show like *A Different World* was actually an example of Black college life. He never even realized when he watched the famed Spike Lee film *School Daze* that a Black college was different from other schools. He just thought he was relating to something that was entertaining—but perhaps it was his familiarity with certain elements of the film that made it more significant to him. Ja'Ron recalls a time in high school when his sister asked him where he was going to go to college. His academic efforts had just started paying off, and he had not even thought about what was beyond those high school classrooms. As a huge college football fan, he thought he would likely apply to big sports schools such as Ohio State or Penn State, but he got to thinking that Black schools like Grambling or Tennessee State should be in the mix as well. As happens in so many families, word got around about these decisions, and the father of one of Ja'Ron's former football teammates reached out to him. This man had served as something of a mentor to Ja'Ron in the past, and found out about his interest in attending a Black university. It was at that time that this gentleman, Reverend Sadler, told him that there was only one place for Ja'Ron—Howard University.

Ja'Ron eventually chose Howard not just because of its great reputation, but because of the draw of living in Washington, D.C. He had never visited Howard, or frankly any other school he had applied to, so he did not know what to expect upon arrival. Once again, like so many college students, after the obligatory parental drop-off, Ja'Ron was simply a deer in headlights. He was overwhelmed by the sheer diversity of all of the Black people around him. He had grown up in a Black neighborhood.

---

[209] See www.blackpast.org.

He had attended a majority-White Catholic school, and this was simply a brand-new experience. What struck him at Howard was that not all Black people were poor or middle class. So many of his classmates where third or fourth-generation college students or had parents who were lawyers and doctors. He quickly developed incredible friendships and became steeped in an education that fed his curiosity, developed his independence, and nurtured the courage that would allow him to tread his own path. It was at Howard University that Ja'Ron became a Republican.

The duality of growing up in a lower-middle-class Black community but attending a diverse Catholic school from kindergarten to the twelfth grade had a huge effect on Ja'Ron's adult life. And this experience permitted Ja'Ron to utilize a heightened critical thinking skill in his transition to college. He intellectually questioned everything, and relied only on himself to confirm the veracity of the many points of view being presented. One moment in particular was immensely impactful on a young Ja'Ron, who up until that time had identified as a Democrat. It was when a very well-known Democratic politician, who happened to be White, came to speak at Howard. Ja'Ron remembers that the politician preached like a Black pastor, and the words seemed more like pandering than any real policy speech. He even recalls one student saying that "he did everything but serve us fried chicken." After that experience, Ja'Ron started to read books like *The Souls of Black Folk* by W. E. B. Du Bois. In that book, Du Bois writes on the notion of a double consciousness—a struggle between the Black identity and the American identity. This struck a particular chord with Ja'Ron, whose family and neighborhood were Black, while his teachers, his coaches, and many of his fellow students were White. He wrestled with the idea that in the White community, he had to repress his Blackness; but in the Black community, he had to repress anything that seemed White. This struggle was externalized even in things like how he spoke—Ja'Ron recalls being picked on for sounding like a "White boy." When Ja'Ron tells the story, he does not hesitate to mention that the kid backed down when he saw just how imposing a figure Ja'Ron could be, but the incident foreshadowed a struggle that he would encounter as a Black Republican as an adult. He was sometimes viewed as an "Uncle Tom" or something of a traitor to his Black community for joining the Republican party.

But none of these experiences took away from Ja'Ron's college experience, or from his development as a servant leader on campus. He engaged in many late-night dorm conversations about how the Black community could be empowered by the next generation. That engagement, coupled with the art and culture of the Black diaspora, opened up something special in him. He recalls that in those days it was described as something of an awakening, as even many Black people were not familiar with all of their people's history. Once awakened, those people were identified as being conscious. Decades later, the term "awakened" would become perverted as the commonly used phrase "woke," whose current context bears little connectivity to its distant derivation.

For Ja'Ron, his awakening centered around the intentionality of action to help advance the Black community as a whole. But what he learned then was that to act on that goal—to change America—he would need to change himself. That is a pretty big realization for a twenty-year-old, and he did not know where to begin. He knew that whatever path he took, it was important to ensure that critical elements of the Black story and Black culture remained at the forefront of his efforts, as it was those kinds of contributions to the American story that make this country so special. So, fast-forwarding almost fifteen years, this first-generation Black college student would get the opportunity to achieve his goal of advancing the Black community, alongside the President of the United States, through what became permanent federal funding for HBCUs.

As has been discussed, the historic importance of HBCUs has been integral to American society, and the Trump administration made efforts to bring these schools onto the main stage of the U.S. government—the White House. Some additional historical perspective may be helpful here. As important as HBCUs have been over the last one hundred and fifty years, it was President Jimmy Carter who first established an executive order to support their funding on a federal level. Versions of that executive order have been rewritten by every president since then, including one involving the creation of a presidential advisory council under President George W. Bush—headed by Jim Cheek, then president of Howard University. Leonard Haynes, who served as assistant secretary at the Department of Education in that Bush administration, recalls the state of HBCUs and the federal government at that time, sharing that although almost $30 billion had been provided to HBCUs over many decades under the Title III program, these institutions had traditionally been ignored on many levels.[210] Haynes would go on to serve on that same presidential HBCU advisory council in the Trump administration, seeking to correct some of the President Barack Obama–era policies that negatively impacted the HBCU community.[211] One of Haynes' criticisms of the Obama administration is its cancellation of the Parent PLUS loan program.[212] According to Haynes, this action removed almost $170 million from the operating capital of HBCUs. As HBCUs rely on federal dollars for 90 percent of their funding through grants and student financial assistance, this "cut HBCUs at the knees."[213] Much of this funding reduction went unreported by the media, but it was seismic for these important institutions.[214]

---

[210] Interview with Dr. Leonard Haynes, August 2022.

[211] Interview with Dr. Leonard Haynes, August 2022.

[212] *"Parent PLUS loans are federal student loans issued directly to parents. The government takes a look at your credit, offers some flexibility in repayment options, and the ability to fill funding gaps after exhausting federal student loans to students, grants, and scholarships."* Reyna Gobel, "What is a Parent PLUS Loan? Eligibility, Interest Rates, Repayment & More," Sallie Mae, March 17, 2022, https://www.salliemae.com/blog/what-is-a-parent-plus-loan/.

[213] Interview with Dr. Leonard Haynes, August 2022.

[214] Interview with Dr. Leonard Haynes, August 2022.

With this new headwind directly in the face of the HBCUs, the stage was set for change in 2017, and that first opportunity came for four schools in the New Orleans and Mississippi areas still feeling the impact of Hurricane Katrina over ten years earlier. These HBCUs—Xavier, Tougaloo, Dillard, and Southern—had been provided federal loans at 1 percent interest as part of their rebuilding efforts.[215] In 2017, they collectively had almost $90 million outstanding on those loans. The schools had struggled to make all of the payments, and had lobbied the Obama administration for financial relief.[216] According to Haynes, these requests did not go anywhere.[217] Once Trump took office, the schools made these requests again, hoping that a new president would mean a different result—and it did. The schools approached the White House Office of Management and Budget (OMB) to forgive the debt held under the HBCU Capital Refinance Program. They were told that dismissal of this debt under the Title III program could only come directly from President Trump.[218] After being briefed on these circumstances by Secretary of Education Betsy DeVos, Ja'Ron, and other key White House advisors, President Trump honored the request, forgiving the entire amount owed by the schools.[219] While there was little to no press associated with this action, the information was shared among the larger HBCU community, which led seventeen other HBCUs to petition the Trump administration for forgiveness of $350 million in federal debt.[220] Once again, the OMB deferred to President Trump. Once again, he was advised by Secretary DeVos, Ja'Ron, and other White House personnel. And once again,

[215] Interview with Dr. Leonard Haynes, August 2022.
[216] Interview with Dr. Leonard Haynes, August 2022.
[217] Interview with Dr. Leonard Haynes, August 2022.
[218] Interview with Dr. Leonard Haynes, August 2022.
[219] Interview with Dr. Leonard Haynes, August 2022.
[220] Interview with Dr. Leonard Haynes, August 2022.

without pomp and circumstance, Trump forgave this debt. And yet, once again, the action received little to no public attention.[221]

Haynes also recalls the very consequential hiring of Jonathan Holifield—a former NFL player and lawyer who lived in the Cincinnati area—to lead the HBCU initiative for the Trump administration. He was technically a Department of Education employee, but answering a call that the HBCU community had been making for decades, he was brought into the White House complex as a member of President Trump's Domestic Policy Council.[222] This action not only ensured that HBCU decision-making was part of Trump's direct domestic agenda, but guaranteed engagement with his other cabinet agencies—as seen when Chris visited HBCUs in North Carolina as acting administrator of the SBA to discuss student training programs in advanced manufacturing. With Ja'Ron, Holifield, and Haynes in place, as well as Johnny Taylor—the former head of the Thurgood Marshall College Fund, now chair of the president's HBCU council—the Trump administration was poised to make its biggest change yet for HBCUs.

In the 1990s, the HBCUs' system oversight and funding was relegated to the Department of Education. That was changed in 2017, when oversight moved to 1600 Pennsylvania Avenue. For over two decades, Congress had been hosting HBCU forums. Having worked on those in his roles on Capitol Hill, Ja'Ron now wanted to coordinate these events out of the White House. Accordingly, he worked alongside Speaker Paul Ryan and Senator Tim Scott to put together an event for HBCU leadership in the White House's Roosevelt Room, with a planned visit by President Trump. This aligned with a recently signed executive order titled White House Initiative to Promote Excellence and Innovation at Historically Black Colleges and Universities, which sought to advance the

---

[221] Interview with Dr. Leonard Haynes, August 2022.
[222] Interview with Dr. Leonard Haynes, August 2022.

mission and functions of these schools.[223] While in the Roosevelt Room, the majority of the HBCU presidents met with the administration's staff to talk about the impact and policies surrounding the executive order, and how its implementation could benefit the HBCU community. At some point during that conversation, a staffer announced that President Trump wanted them to join him in the Oval Office.

Well, as you may know, the White House is not a very large place, and the Oval Office—while one of the most powerful places on the planet—is not very large either. It is of course a unique opportunity to be invited into the Oval Office, but a couple of dozen visitors plus staff and the press can make it a bit cramped. On that day, once everyone had entered, President Trump made some remarks. Some of these were precursors to his decision to fully fund the HBCUs on a permanent basis, as opposed to approving funding from year to year, as had been done by prior administrations. But while the historic importance of a

---

[223] *"Historically black colleges and universities (HBCUs) have made, and continue to make, extraordinary contributions to the general welfare and prosperity of our country. Established by visionary leaders, America's HBCUs have, for more than 150 years, produced many of our Nation's leaders in business, government, academia, and the military, and have helped create a black middle class. The Nation's more than 100 HBCUs are located in 20 States, the District of Columbia, and the U.S. Virgin Islands, and serve more than 300,000 undergraduate, graduate, and professional students. These institutions are important engines of economic growth and public service, and they are proven ladders of intergenerational advancement. A White House Initiative on HBCUs would: advance America's full human potential; foster more and better opportunities in higher education; strengthen the capacity of HBCUs to provide the highest-quality education; provide equitable opportunities for HBCUs to participate in Federal programs; and increase the number of college-educated Americans who feel empowered and able to advance the common good at home and abroad."* "White House Initiative to Promote Excellence and Innovation at Historically Black Colleges and Universities," Executive Office of the President, https://www.federalregister.gov/documents/2017/03/03/2017-04357/ white-house-initiative-to-promote-excellence-and-innovation-at-historically-black-colleges-and.

U.S. president's meeting with almost all of the HBCU leadership on the verge of permanent funding for these institutions should have been the news story, the media picture that frequently remains from that event is a shot of Senior Advisor Kellyanne Conway climbing onto a sofa to get a picture of this amazing gathering, because that was the only vantage point available given the number of people in the room.[224] That picture has appeared in the media countless times since then, and often either provides no context for the circumstances or seeks to show her as being so casual that she would put her feet on the sofa in the Oval Office. The reality, as mentioned, is that this moment should have been remembered as setting the stage for President Trump to provide permanent funding for HBCUs, but as expressed by advisory board chair Johnny Taylor:

> *This was something that, frankly, the black college community assumed would have been easily accomplished with the first African-American president, and after over eight years of repeated requests, to think that within 45 days of his presidency we were able to convene all of the [HBCU] presidents in the Oval Office [Monday] and [on Tuesday] a subset of us were able to come back and sign the executive order the same day that the [president] is preparing for first State of the Union address. [That] gives this tremendous importance. It's bittersweet, but at the end of the day, we focus on the sweet.*[225]

---

[224] Kalhan Rosenblatt, "Kellyanne Conway Explains Why She Was Kneeling on Oval Office Couch," NBC News, March 1, 2017, https://www.nbcnews.com/news/us-news/kellyanne-conway-explains-why-she-was-kneeling-oval-office-couch-n727576.

[225] Mark W. Wright, "Trump Signs Executive Order on HBCUs, Says Schools Will Be Priority in His White House," Andscape, March 1, 2017, https://andscape.com/features/trump-signs-executive-order-on-hbcus/

Finally securing this funding positioned HBCUs to turn to the private sector to form the right partnerships, so that now they could be more independent—similar to other elite institutions of higher education.[226] Unfortunately, this was one of the last photos of HBCU leaders at the Trump White House.[227] It is not because the administration did not keep supporting them—because in fact it did—but because certain media personalities characterized the White House Oval Office event as a simple photo opportunity, which discouraged future public stakeholder engagement.[228] But, as mentioned, the assistance continued with various initiatives, such as Trump's authorization of $50 million to assist Howard University during its own financial difficulties.[229]

As Haynes points out, the key for HBCUs going forward is to ensure that they have a plan to remain relevant and spend their funding in a way that advances their larger educational calling.[230] That includes investing in research and development, and creating operational plans that make a compelling case that they will continue to serve as cutting-edge facilities for the advancement of underserved Black communities.[231] Haynes fears that if they do not get their financial and directional houses in order, it will be difficult for HBCUs to sustain the headwinds of change across the educational sector.[232] To President Trump's credit, his administration sought to help them do just that and get organized for the future. This was very much exemplified in a presentation that the chancellor of North Carolina Agricultural and Technical State University presented to Secretary DeVos on a trip to the school, when he set forth a vision that sought to incorporate his students into the various industry inno-

---

[226] Interview with Dr. Leonard Haynes, August 2022.
[227] Interview with Dr. Leonard Haynes, August 2022.
[228] Interview with Dr. Leonard Haynes, August 2022.
[229] Interview with Dr. Leonard Haynes, August 2022.
[230] Interview with Dr. Leonard Haynes, August 2022.
[231] Interview with Dr. Leonard Haynes, August 2022.
[232] Interview with Dr. Leonard Haynes, August 2022.

vations across their state.[233] According to Haynes, the state of HBCUs is something of a question mark under the Biden administration to date. As of this writing, no new funds have been spent on these schools, and the funds provided to date were simply part of the general higher education dollars appropriated by the pandemic-driven CARES Act.[234] And remember the importance of the HBCU liaison position that Jonathan Holifield held at the White House during the Trump administration? Haynes says that role has since been relegated back to the Department of Education's offices in southwest Washington, D.C.[235]

As you can see, a variety of approaches to education and workforce development have been undertaken to address the many questions of the market failure of the underserved. While some are intentional and seek to historically advance a pathway for so many from these communities, many of them have been fleeting, piecemeal, or not constructed in a way that would allow for the necessary flexibility and adaptability to the circumstances. Unlike government programs, corporate approaches to these problems, or at least approaches informed by leaders of public-private partnerships, can account for the present and plan for their future efforts with data-driven economic rigor. That is in part why the Pledge to America's Workers was so widely adopted. It addressed the need to connect workers with companies and served as something of a facilitating bridge between the two—a bridge that also could identify and provide access to specific and relevant training programs. Further, institutions like HBCUs have been so critical to our country for so many decades, and ensuring that they are equipped to navigate both our national challenges and those specific to institutions of higher learning will be paramount to ensuring their long-term sustainability.

---

[233] Interview with Dr. Leonard Haynes, August 2022.
[234] Interview with Dr. Leonard Haynes, August 2022.
[235] Interview with Dr. Leonard Haynes, August 2022.

CHAPTER **FIVE**

Entrepreneurship, Economic Development, and the Trump Administration's Response: Opportunity Zones and the Paycheck Protection Program

Poverty and economic development are inextricably linked. Oftentimes, intentions for economic development arrive via the government or private sector firms, and while their efforts result in an outward picture of economic growth, those who resided in the geographic area before the economic activity simply become poor people living in a rich neighborhood that they can no longer afford. This in no way disparages the concept of economic development. Rather, it stresses that true economic development must be holistic and take a view that does not simply assume prosperity, but takes concrete action to intentionally support it.

The subtlety of this point is best illustrated by President Lincoln's views as a young man. As a surveyor in Illinois, he drew plans for a town he called Huron. While the town was never built, it combined the use of canals and railroads to serve as a hub of transport for the agricultural products of Illinois farmers.[236] He saw that the ability to transport these products to the vibrant port cities of New Orleans and beyond would allow these Illinois families to "ascend the economic ladder."[237] This concept would be included in one of his early state legislative campaigns and would translate into his support for the transcontinental railroad during his presidency.[238] This example illustrates an important distinction in Lincoln's view on economic development. Unlike President Lyndon Johnson with his War on Poverty, for example, which focused on (albeit well-intended) government-subsidized programs, Lincoln embraced an ideology more consistent with the idea that *a rising tide lifts all boats*.

While the issue of poverty is omnipresent, many politicians avoid providing a specific strategy to address it. The national average for those in poverty is just over 10 percent, but that number is higher for minority groups and other underserved communities, and in fact, it more than doubles for Black people.[239] As has been discussed, offshoring and certain components of globalization undoubtedly have played a role, and access to consolidated banking capital and federal resources has served as a limiting factor as well. For example, rural areas historically have faced economic development challenges, as seen in responsive government proposals from Theodore Roosevelt in the early 1900s and in his cousin Franklin Roosevelt's 1933 Agricultural Adjustment Act, which concentrated on farming without accounting for the diversity of needs and resources.[240]

---

236 "Lincolnomics: How President Lincoln Constructed the Great American Economy," *History Unplugged Podcast*, May 25, 2021.

237 "Lincolnomics: How President Lincoln Constructed the Great American Economy."

238 "Lincolnomics: How President Lincoln Constructed the Great American Economy."

239 Edward Royce, *Poverty and Power* (Rowman and Littlefield Publishing, 2019), 3.

240 Olugbenga Ajilore and Caius Z. Willingham, "The Path to Rural Resilience in America," Center for American Progress, September 21, 2020, https://www.

Some political commentators have expressed that the Department of Agriculture is ostensibly multiple agencies that can be faced with bureaucratic challenges in implementing a central strategy, suggesting that a rural opportunity administration should be created to effectuate more impactful economic development.[241] The argument is that something like this could promote the development of health, education, and manufacturing opportunities in rural areas, and the jobs that come with it.[242] Some make the point that without such a commitment, young people will have no choice other than to move to urban areas—forcing them to abandon their communities to pursue any real economic opportunity.[243] Various administrations have sought to address this issue in rural communities in one way or another, but approaches, goals, and priorities change and the pendulum of progress ultimately swings back.[244] This concept of changing priorities was aptly captured in a 1967 National Advisory Commission on Rural Poverty report entitled *The People Left Behind*.[245] It stated that "some of our rural programs, especially farm and vocational agriculture programs, are relics from an earlier era. They were developed in a period during which the welfare of farm families was equated with the well-being of rural communities and of all rural people. This no longer is so."[246]

As has been discussed, the programs of the New Deal certainly had a significant impact on communities all across America, but an undeniable result was the setting of something of a precedent for government

---

americanprogress.org/article/path-rural-resilience-america/.

[241] Ajilore and Willingham, "The Path to Rural Resilience in America."

[242] Ajilore and Willingham, "The Path to Rural Resilience in America."

[243] Ajilore and Willingham, "The Path to Rural Resilience in America."

[244] Ajilore and Willingham, "The Path to Rural Resilience in America."

[245] Edward T. Breathitt, "The People Left Behind, A Report by the President's National Advisory Commission on Rural Poverty," U.S. Government Printing Office, September 1967, https://files.eric.ed.gov/fulltext/ED016543.pdf.

[246] Ajilore and Willingham, "The Path to Rural Resilience in America."

intervention to support certain economic and social components of America.[247] This precedent was used by many of President Franklin Roosevelt's successors to develop urban areas as well, often involving the de facto relocation of lower to middle-income residents to achieve redevelopment objectives.[248] Over time, increased unemployment due to manufacturing losses and other reduced opportunities for these groups led to an eroding tax base and resident displacement, as seen in cities such as Youngstown and Cleveland in Ohio as well as Wheeling, West Virginia, and Pittsburgh, Pennsylvania, in the late 1970s and 1980s.[249] These and other factors can undermine law and order, and can exacerbate flight from these cities by residents who can no longer tolerate these conditions.

In 1980, Jack Kemp introduced to America the concept of enterprise zones, a tool for urban revitalization to strengthen economies through a combination of tax cuts, deregulation, and federal grants.[250] This concept had been developed by Geoffrey Howe of Great Britain in the 1970s and was embraced by Prime Minister Margaret Thatcher, as well as her counterpart in the United States, President Ronald Reagan.[251] Developed in the U.S. as an alternative to substantive public investment, this plan was criticized by some Democrats, who said that its scope was too limited, its impact would be minimal, and its enactment might jeopardize federal funding for these areas.[252] With a federal deadlock, states developed their

---

[247] "Forty Years of Urban Economic Development: A Retrospective," International Economic Council, February 2008, https://www.iedconline.org/clientuploads/Downloads/history/Forty_Years_Urban_Economic_Development.pdf.

[248] "Forty Years of Urban Economic Development: A Retrospective."

[249] "Forty Years of Urban Economic Development: A Retrospective."

[250] Michael J. Rich and Robert P. Stoker, *Collaborative Governance for Urban Revitalization: Lessons from Empowerment Zones* (Cornell University Press, 2014), 26–27.

[251] Rich and Stoker, *Collaborative Governance for Urban Revitalization: Lessons from Empowerment Zones*, 26–27.

[252] Rich and Stoker, *Collaborative Governance for Urban Revitalization: Lessons from Empowerment Zones*, 30.

own enterprise zone programs, and by 1993, more than three thousand zones had been established in forty states. Programs varied from state to state, with some including direct loans and venture capital access. Although the federal enterprise zone concept was briefly resurrected in 1992, President George H.W. Bush vetoed it before Bill Clinton took office—but Clinton would develop his own take on this tool based on his experience with enterprise zones as governor of Arkansas.[253]

It is important to note how Jack Kemp came to embrace this approach. As discussed with this book's authors, Kemp's son Jimmy explained that his father's political philosophy came down to advancing the American idea, an idea whose source was the Declaration of Independence itself, particularly the words: "We hold these truths to be self-evident, that all men are created equal, that they are endowed by their Creator with certain unalienable Rights, that among these are Life, Liberty and the pursuit of Happiness.—That to secure these rights, Governments are instituted among Men, deriving their just powers from the consent of the governed..."[254] In Jack Kemp's view, every human had inalienable rights and inestimable value, and was blessed with the gift of self-governance. As the conservative radio host and writer Dennis Prager states, "The bigger the government, the smaller the citizen," and that is exactly how Kemp felt about the potential of all Americans.[255] His American idea—or our American identity—was based on this concept of self-governance, and the expansion of government only moves us away from the intentions of the American experiment so that the people are unable to govern themselves. Jimmy further explained that the more that people focus on

---

[253] Rich and Stoker, *Collaborative Governance for Urban Revitalization: Lessons from Empowerment Zones*, 26–27.

[254] Declaration of Independence, United States National Archives, https://www.archives.gov/founding-docs/declaration-transcript.

[255] Interview with Jimmy Kemp, August 2022.

government as the answer to our challenges, the more they cede to the government the power that the founders intended them to have.[256]

Kemp saw enterprise zones as focusing power in a very local way, allowing the market to truly dictate what needed to happen there.[257] Embracing the work of thought leaders such as Milton Friedman, Kemp believed in classical free market economics—that is, that people will engage when incentives are present. Capital gains were not part of the enterprise zone program; removal of those capital gains could serve as that incentive.[258] Kemp's view was that incorporating an additional calculation into an already complicated tax code would give the government the power to regulate and prioritize programming, as opposed to simply letting the market—investors, businesses, and the community—determine the highest and best use of the opportunity.[259] As will be discussed, this approach embracing no capital gains is comparable to the ten-year holding period of the opportunity zone program; however, the lack of a capital gains requirement upon investment was unique then and is frankly still unique now.[260]

In speaking with the authors of this book about his father's focus on underserved communities, Jimmy shared that his father openly referred to himself as a "bleeding heart conservative." He recalled that the origins of this began with Jack seeing his own father start a small delivery business in Hollywood, California, called the California Delivery Service.[261] With its ambitious name for a two-person operation, the company became the lifeblood of the Kemp family, and young Jack knew that much

---

[256] Interview with Jimmy Kemp, August 2022.
[257] Interview with Jimmy Kemp, August 2022.
[258] Interview with Jimmy Kemp, August 2022.
[259] Interview with Jimmy Kemp, August 2022.
[260] Interview with Jimmy Kemp, August 2022.
[261] Interview with Jimmy Kemp, August 2022.

of his future was tied to its success.[262] And it is well-known that Jack Kemp had great success—certainly as a politician, but first as a quarterback in the NFL. In fact, he had James "Shack" Harris—the first Black man to start a football season as a quarterback—as a teammate.[263] As this was the 1960s, Kemp's Buffalo Bills traveled to many cities where racist policies were the norm—including those specifying that Black people had to stay in separate hotels from White people in places such as New Orleans and elsewhere.[264]

Jimmy also shared his father's recollections of seeing his Black teammates' parents being forced to sit in an entirely different section of the stadiums where the team played. As Jimmy put it, his father's view could be summed up with the idea that "there but for the grace of God go I"—meaning that but for the color of his skin, Kemp may not have gotten the opportunities he had, even though he knew that the true mark of a person was anchored in their character, merit, and performance.[265] Jack Kemp abhorred the original sin of slavery and Jim Crow laws, and wanted to ensure that economic equality of opportunity was present for all people—regardless of race.[266] In Jack Kemp's own words, "the American idea was never that everyone would be leveled to the same position in life. The American idea was that each individual should have the same opportunity to rise as high as his effort and initiative and God-given talent could carry him. If you were born to be a master carpenter, or a mezzo-soprano—or even a pro football player—here in America you could make it…"[267] The foundation that bears his name celebrates Jack Kemp's legacy as being part of the same tradition as Abraham Lincoln—embracing that idea that Americans are providential heirs of a "nation,

262 Interview with Jimmy Kemp, August 2022.
263 Interview with Jimmy Kemp, August 2022.
264 Interview with Jimmy Kemp, August 2022.
265 Interview with Jimmy Kemp, August 2022.
266 Interview with Jimmy Kemp, August 2022.
267 Jack Kemp Foundation, https://www.jackkempfoundation.org/.

conceived in liberty and dedicated to the proposition that all men are created equal." [268]

A successor of sorts to Kemp's enterprise zones was authorized by the Omnibus Budget Reconciliation Act of 1993, referred to as empowerment zones. A product of the Clinton administration, they sought to provide tax incentives to businesses located within areas experiencing the highest poverty and most significant unemployment rates. The incentives included an annual tax credit of $3,000 per employee, an eligible equipment deduction of up to $30,000, as well as EZ Facility bonds, which were tax-exempt private-purpose bonds to be used for commercial development. [269] The program began with just under one hundred designated areas. [270]

Along with the identification of metrics around local poverty and unemployment, successful zone applications included a written commitment to a specific vision of change, an overview of the community-based partnerships in place and the stakeholders to be engaged, a plan for job training and capital access for residents, and an approach to community economic development that accounted for certain physical and environmental factors. [271] The data on the impact of these zones demonstrated minimal results, with researchers noting that not only was governance a critical component to their success or failure, but a robust study period of the underlying social problems in an area as opposed to intelligent guesses was critical. [272] As an example, while the Atlanta empowerment zone program made some progress, it was roundly criticized not only because county and state governments were not significantly active in its

---

[268] Jack Kemp Foundation, https://www.jackkempfoundation.org/.

[269] "Forty Years of Urban Economic Development: A Retrospective."

[270] "Forty Years of Urban Economic Development: A Retrospective."

[271] "Forty Years of Urban Economic Development: A Retrospective."

[272] Rich and Stoker, *Collaborative Governance for Urban Revitalization: Lessons from Empowerment Zones*, 30.

development, but because corporate partners and relevant business associations did not engage and provide input—undercutting the impacts.[273]

The successes and failures of some of the urban economic programs over the past several decades offer lessons to learn. Consistent themes include the need for a comprehensive strategy to address the conditions of the underserved, coordination and empowerment of an entity to achieve that goal, mobilization of residents in the particular community, and a substantive role for state governments in the process.[274] Of course, private sector engagement is critical. Whether that be direct engagement or engagement based on incentivized private investment structures, they must be motivated to participate in local economic development. Nonprofit partners who hold key insights and can help establish local buy-in also must be engaged. All of this can truly coalesce around a very local approach that accounts for what products or services will help that locality, or that may even give stakeholders an opportunity to be engaged in further domestic commerce or global trade. As one stakeholder puts it, "There is no Marshall Plan for Urban Economic Development."[275] But of course, there is no time like the present to consider how to develop and implement such a critical plan.

A good example of an intentional commitment to economic development can be found in North Carolina, a state historically known for its textile manufacturing. As part of the globalization of the 1990s, significant outsourcing of textile production occurred in the country—a large percentage of it in North Carolina. But while almost an entire generation lost skills in the development of fabric textiles and the apparel industry due to globalization, experts still remained in the state. And schools such

---

273 Rich and Stoker, *Collaborative Governance for Urban Revitalization: Lessons from Empowerment Zones*, 26–27.
274 See generally Rich and Stoker, *Collaborative Governance for Urban Revitalization: Lessons from Empowerment Zones*.
275 "Forty Years of Urban Economic Development: A Retrospective."

as North Carolina State University's Wilson College of Textiles and the community college system's Manufacturing Solutions Center saw an opportunity to work with their students and large retailers to reteach these skills, create jobs through advanced manufacturing, and cut time and costs from supply chains—many of which included factories in Asia.[276] This vision, coupled with private and public sector support, has led to the launching of hundreds of entrepreneurial ventures in a rural area. In turn, these ventures have produced venture capital investment, fabric patents, and burgeoning employment opportunities throughout the state.

In 2018, coauthor Chris and Matt Stanton, an old friend from high school who led government affairs for a large apparel firm, got to talking about the small-business ecosystems that were developing around some of the trade needs for the apparel companies. In the wake of globalization and its impact on North Carolina manufacturing, many large apparel companies had to source much of their product from other countries, increasing the time it took to physically get products into the American market. The problem with that model is that modern-day American customers have an on-demand mentality. If they like something, they will click online and order it. If it is not available or delayed, their attention and their order will likely go elsewhere. The answer to the apparel companies' dilemma is to make the materials closer to home, but that strategy presents firms with many challenges, including a lack of access to resources and trained workers.

That gap presented an interesting entrepreneurial opportunity. Chris began to learn more about the Manufacturing Solutions Center (MSC), which is an initiative composed of two of North Carolina's community college systems—Catawba and Galveston.[277] Working in partnership

---

[276] "Manufacturing Solutions Center," Catawba Valley Community College, https://www.cvcc.edu/CCE/Manufacturing_Solutions_Center/index.cfm.

[277] *"The mission of the Manufacturing Solutions Center is to help US manufacturers increase sales, improve quality and improve efficiency to create or retain jobs. This is*

with North Carolina State University (NCSU), MSC developed an entrepreneurial ecosystem for a few hundred small businesses—mostly in the apparel industry. This effort provided these businesses with space, mentoring, and other business assistance, much of which was teamed with student and research expertise on advanced manufacturing from NCSU. One of the questions that always comes up with any advanced manufacturing initiative is whether heavy automation will minimize job opportunities. The reality is that many of the jobs are developed on the technology, engineering, and coding end. As such, you may not see the people on the factory floor, but the human element to making manufacturing processes work and keeping them working well is critical.

Exposure to this ecosystem gave Chris more vision into the many opportunities for shared services for budding entrepreneurs. One of these

---

accomplished by: Enhancing and improving products through research and development; Creating prototypes for new, innovative offerings; Analyzing new materials to enhance structure and programs; Testing products for reliable content and quality; Training personnel for lean manufacturing processes and supply chain efficiencies; Providing a forum for rollout of new 21ˢᵗ century technologies; Providing hands-on guidance for international marketing, sales and military procurement; Providing photo-realistic renderings and visualizations; Advocating Industry; and Aiding entrepreneurs in success. The Manufacturing Solutions Center is a new undertaking at Catawba Valley Community College. Building on a solid experience in outreach to traditional manufacturing, Manufacturing Solutions Center is prepared to move companies forward. Manufacturing, once the backbone of the American economy, has shrunk. Other parts of the world with lower labor costs, fewer regulations, and stronger support services have attracted production once based in the U.S. Some manufacturing however, is thriving. Companies with superior products and savvy marketing strategies are growing. The Manufacturing Solutions Center is a facility where innovative concepts may be put through design, or the research and development processes. It's where products and prototypes are tested; manufacturing processes are fine-tuned and accurate cost and product studies are performed. All of these services are available to manufacturers to help them stay at the forefront of their industry." "Our Mission," Manufacturing Solutions Center, https://www.manufacturingsolutionscenter.org/mission.html.

opportunities is referred to as a makerspace, which can be anything from a two-person garage project to a vast warehouse that provides classes on hardware and free community access to things like 3D printers and laser-cutting equipment. While touring one of the latter in Baltimore, Chris was told a story about some of the makerspace's recent class attendees. These particular individuals had been learning about stonecutting, and the instructor shared a story with Chris that would stick with him forever.

The story centered on a few young people who were in their late teens and from the Baltimore area. A few weeks into their training, they approached the instructor with a business idea: starting a company that would make low-cost headstones. They shared that the rationale for this business idea was that they had lost so many friends to gang violence, and their friends' families could not find affordable options with which to mark the burial sites of their loved ones. Addressing heartbreaking realities like these requires both intentional and creative thinking by policy makers.

Shortly thereafter, in his role leading the SBA, exposure to the possibility of makerspaces led Chris to establish the SBA Makerspace Training, Collaboration and Hiring (MaTCH) pilot competition to fund makerspace ecosystems all across the country—seeking to embolden these entrepreneurial ecosystems and advance workforce development opportunities in communities all across the country.[278] Working closely

---

[278] *"Makerspaces are collaborative places where people work to solve problems by sharing ideas and experiences and developing new skills. Many of them offer tools like 3D printers, laser cutters, soldering irons and sewing machines for community use. We at the SBA believe these makerspaces have the resources and ingenuity necessary to solve the problem small businesses face. They are uniquely positioned to boost workforce development by fostering vocational education, apprenticeships and entrepreneurship. And we hope this competition will both empower creative thinking and strengthen the link between these spaces and their local communities. The ultimate goal – expanded job skills will offer working families a pathway to the middle class,*

with makerspace veterans, a key makerspace trade association, and the National Association of Manufacturing, the program's organizers helped to catalyze organizations in North Carolina, Puerto Rico, Missouri, New Hampshire, New York, Indiana, California, New Jersey, Pennsylvania, and Oklahoma.[279] While much more attention needs to be given to these facilities that generate entrepreneurship and workforce training, this unique MaTCH program laid the groundwork for many special economic development opportunities, including an incredible business that not only provided job training on carpentry, but did so in order to produce low-cost furniture for residents moving into affordable housing.[280] In short, the impact of these makerspaces is most notably expressed by one young person in Buffalo who explained that she did not know where she would be without this opportunity and that it was the best thing she had ever done;[281] while another young man showed that exposure to these programs could serve as a force-multiplier in communities, stating that he "came in like in a shell and really quiet, and now [was] out speaking

and a skilled workforce will drive economic growth that benefits us all." Chris Pilkerton, "MaTCH Competition Aims to Ignite Workforce Development," U.S. Small Business Administration, May 28, 2019, https://www.sba.gov/blog/match-competition-aims-ignite-workforce-development.

[279] "Acting Administrator Pilkerton Announces Makerspace Training, Collaboration and Hiring (MaTCH) Pilot Competition Winners," U.S. Small Business Administration, August 20, 2019, https://www.prnewswire.com/news-releases/acting-administrator-pilkerton-announces-makerspace-training-collaboration-and-hiring-match-pilot-competition-winners-300904480.html.

[280] Pilkerton, "Acting SBA Chief Chris Pilkerton: Why the Small Business Administration Is Investing in Local Entrepreneurs," Fox Business, October 29, 2019, https://www.foxbusiness.com/small-business/acting-sba-chief-chris-pilkerton-why-small-business-administration-investing-local-entrepreneurs.

[281] Pilkerton, "Acting SBA Chief Chris Pilkerton: Why the Small Business Administration Is Investing in Local Entrepreneurs."

out for other people like [him] around the country, as an ambassador for [the] program."[282]

Most policy ideas require an anchor component, and much of the small-business-ecosystem work was tied to an accomplishment of the Trump White House—the implementation of opportunity zones, often referred to as OZs. This concept was part of the 2017 Tax Cuts and Jobs Act, and in summary sought to generate economic development and job creation by providing a tax incentive for investments directly in distressed areas.[283] To ensure that these distressed areas could serve as a component of the larger economic strategy for states, the governors selected the regions to be designated as OZs in their states.[284] These areas, which aligned with eligible low-income census tracts, resulted in the creation of nearly nine thousand OZs where new or existing businesses could relocate and develop.[285] The investors' contributions, which were required to be invested in Qualified Opportunity Funds (QOFs), resulted in tax deferrals and capital gain reductions that increased over

[282] Matt Glynn, "Foundry Gets Recognition, $100,000 from SBA to Support Job Training," *Buffalo News*, August 30, 2019, https://buffalonews.com/business/local/foundry-gets-recognition-100-000-from-sba-to-support-job-training/article_0f1faa44-d013-549e-8c05-0c9d242fa588.html.

[283] "Opportunity Zones," Internal Revenue Service, November 18, 2022, https://www.irs.gov/credits-deductions/businesses/opportunity-zones#:~:text=Opportunity%20Zones%20were%20created%20under,zones%20through%20Qualified%20Opportunity%20Funds.

[284] "Opportunity Zone Best Practices Report to the President from the White House Opportunity and Revitalization Council," May 2020, https://opportunityzones.hud.gov/sites/opportunityzones.hud.gov/files/documents/OZ_Best_Practices_Report.pdf

[285] "Opportunity Zone Best Practices Report to the President from the White House Opportunity and Revitalization Council," May 2020, https://opportunityzones.hud.gov/sites/opportunityzones.hud.gov/files/documents/OZ_Best_Practices_Report.pdf.

the life of the investment.[286] Through these incentives, the OZ program sought to attract private sector capital, and in a manner that encouraged market-based participation by both investors and the businesses located in the zones. The impacts would then be felt by the residents of the areas, both in increased job opportunities and community development.

The White House Council of Economic Advisers put out a report that highlighted some of the early successes of OZs—showing that QOFs raised nearly $75 billion and estimating that approximately two-thirds of that amount likely would not have found its way into the designated communities without such a program.[287] The data also showed that the program led to the creation of eight hundred thousand to 1.2 million jobs, as well as additional job creation and positive spillover impact in areas not officially designated as OZs.[288]

So how did this all come about? In 2017, President Trump sought a meaningful and practical way to demonstrate a commitment to underserved communities. Probably more than with most presidents, critics were at his door daily on the issues impacting these communities. To show his commitment, President Trump engaged with a trusted policy maker—Senator Tim Scott. Scott had grown up in South Carolina, and as a conservative Black man, he had been at the center of these issues his entire life. That partnership led to the OZ brainchild and its

---

[286] "*A QOF is an investment vehicle that files either a partnership or corporate federal income tax return, is organized for the purpose of investing in QOZ property and elects to self-certify as a Qualified Opportunity Fund.*" "Qualified Opportunity Funds Questions," Internal Revenue Service, November 10, 2022, https://www.irs.gov/credits-deductions/opportunity-zones-frequently-asked-questions#qualifiedfaqs.

[287] "New Report Highlights the Positive Impact of Opportunity Zones," August 24, 2020, https://waysandmeans.house.gov/new-report-highlights-the-positive-impact-of-opportunity-zones/ (referencing Council of Economic Advisors Report 2020 on opportunity zones).

[288] "New Report Highlights the Positive Impact of Opportunity Zones."

implementation. As Trump stated, "Our goal is to ensure that America's great new prosperity is broadly shared by all of our citizens. We are drawing investment into neglected and underserved communities of America so that all Americans, regardless of ZIP code, have access to the American Dream."[289]

The implementation of the OZ program was deemed to be an action that could be taken to lift up these areas in a conservative and market-based way. That said, it was not going to be easy. A number of groups on the left were jockeying for legislative language in the eventual bill—all of which claimed that their programs would lead to the impact that both Trump and Scott were seeking. Further, certain groups on the right had been seeking tax reform for decades, and did not necessarily want to create a hurdle for a new, unproven program that could derail it. Every bill needs a champion, and while Scott was in the Senate, the House champion was Representative Pat Tiberi, the number-two-ranking Republican on the House Ways and Means Committee—the critical committee for any kind of tax bill. As it happened, Tiberi resigned to run for governor, which seemed to stall the potential success of the bill in the House, but fortunately, Speaker Paul Ryan joined in this effort and worked with Trump and Scott to advance the cause, which was something of a next-generation vision of Ryan's former mentor Jack Kemp. Ryan proudly supported the bill, stating, "…on the poverty issues. People don't really report this too much but social impact bonds, opportunity zones, I think our members have gotten more attuned to this issue. It's the stuff that [community development leader and founder of the Woodson

---

[289] Dave Boyer, "Trump Signs Executive Order Promoting 'Opportunity Zones' in distressed towns," AP News, December 13, 2018, originally published in *The Washington Times*, https://apnews.com/article/fe13b9308a4a702690f4b61b8d 9b6b1f.

Center] Bob Woodson and I preach about. It's the stuff I learned from Jack Kemp."[290]

The OZ implementation took approximately two years. This time allowed media reports to gain traction, saying that this program was simply a real estate development loophole and did not give the governors many examples of how to tailor it to advance projects for underserved communities. In fact, many of the projects that got funded initially did advance neighborhood welfare and gentrification, as projects that already were going to get done did get done—but faster. And of course, due to the origins of the program, many liberal governors and big-city mayors were not keen to promote its impact in a public way. At the end of the day, every issue and every piece of legislation has a protagonist and antagonist—just like the basic framework of any novel. The world of developing policy to support the underserved is no different. You would think that bipartisanship would be easier, but the politics can often be messier because success can result in votes being taken away from one side. It's sort of Politics 101, however, when you are talking about an impact on generations of families, you must be creative and retain only what has proven to be effective, and incorporate that into a new blueprint.

One type of institution that has been particularly impactful for underserved communities and certainly can play a significant role in the OZ policy world is community development financial institutions, also known as CDFIs. While not exactly the same as a bank, at a high level, a CDFI could be described as something similar, in that it is designed to support access to capital for underserved communities as its mission. Established as part of the Community Development Banking and Financial Institutions Act of 1994, and signed into law by President Bill Clinton, these institutions are certified under a Department of Treasury

---

[290] Washington Post Live, "Transcript: The Daily 202 with House Speaker Paul Ryan," November 30, 2018, https://www.washingtonpost.com/washington-post-live/2018/11/30/transcript-daily-with-house-speaker-paul-ryan/.

program and are typically licensed by the states in which they principally conduct their lending business. The program covers a variety of areas, such as small business, housing, community facilities, and other associated elements of underfunded communities.[291]

CDFIs are particularly adept at serving the economically disadvantaged and other underserved populations, as their financial products and operations are typically specialized to ensure usability by these communities. Their products often are more flexible, and their credit-risk tolerance usually is higher than that of a traditional bank, which speaks to their origins and functional purpose.[292] Often in partnership with banks and other private sector entities, these CDFIs can offer their customers technical assistance to advance their understanding of the application of the capital, including on topics such as loan counseling, business planning, and homebuying.[293] The CDFIs receive a direct distribution of federal government funds, but often secure capital by partnering with banks as part of the Community Reinvestment Act (CRA) program, as well as with impact donors and philanthropists.[294] Banks often work with the CDFI community to meet their regulatory requirements under the CRA, as set forth by the key banking regulator, the Office of the Comptroller of the Currency. The CRA program mandates that banks engage in activities that are significantly impactful to the underserved, such as providing access to CDFI loans, deposits, equity-equivalent investments,

---

[291] "Bank Partnerships With Community Development Financial Institutions and Benefits of CDFI Certification," Office of the Comptroller of the Currency, September 2019, https://www.occ.gov/publications-and-resources/publications/community-affairs/community-developments-fact-sheets/pub-fact-sheet-bank-partnerships-with-cdfis.pdf.

[292] "Bank Partnerships With Community Development Financial Institutions and Benefits of CDFI Certification."

[293] "Bank Partnerships With Community Development Financial Institutions and Benefits of CDFI Certification."

[294] "Bank Partnerships With Community Development Financial Institutions and Benefits of CDFI Certification."

loan referrals, and technical support (for instance, as related to product development and standards, marketing, and board service).[295]

As has been mentioned, Chris and Ja'Ron worked hand in glove, beginning in March 2020. Chris had a strong knowledge of SBA capabilities, and Ja'Ron was an expert at handling the congressional and White House levers. They worked alongside members of the National Economic Council, the Department of Treasury, Ivanka Trump, and other key partners within the administration to advance funding for all small businesses as part of the Paycheck Protection Program. This advancement included efforts to ensure access to capital for Minority Depository Institutions (MDIs) and CDFIs—organizations that so often receive lip service from some officials, but rarely have the seat at the table that is required to highlight access to capital for the underbanked. In conjunction with the Department of Treasury and SBA leaders, Chris and Ja'Ron were able to play a role in President Trump's setting aside billions of PPP dollars to be lent by MDIs and CDFIs, so that their customers could have equitable access to funds to maintain their workforces.

The conversations surrounding these efforts were not always easy. The federal government was doing a lot in 2020 to ensure the physical and economic health of the American people, and Chris and Ja'Ron got into their fair share of policy dustups behind closed doors so that the administration would have a clear and executable approach to helping the underserved. But the conversations were not about just PPP funding—health, economic, and educational programs also were examined to maximize support for the underserved communities, and Chris and Ja'Ron worked closely with the Office of Management and Budget to scrub every dollar that could be repurposed for economic development. During that time, with the engagement of White House colleagues Steve Smith and William Crozier, Chris and Ja'Ron initiated dozens

---

[295] "Bank Partnerships With Community Development Financial Institutions and Benefits of CDFI Certification."

of calls with Democratic and Republican mayors and local economic development officials to see where federal programs could be redeployed or federal regulations could be reconsidered to maximize much-needed revenues and job creation in these towns and cities.

Alongside these calls with government officials, Chris and Ja'Ron held countless conversations with private sector icons like Bob Johnson (founder of the Black Entertainment Network), Robert Smith (founder of Vista Equity Partners), artist Ice Cube, and John Hope Bryant (founder of Operation HOPE), in order to create bipartisan approaches through which public-private partnerships could be built and scaled. They consistently conducted webinars for any relevant group to which they could connect to ensure that minority-owned businesses understood how to navigate this program to protect their workers and weather the pandemic. Groups such as the National Minority Supplier Diversity Council (NMSDC) and the U.S. Black Chambers were Chris and Ja'Ron's frequent partners in this effort, and the list grew throughout the spring and summer of 2020.

As part of this process, tremendous feedback was received from all kinds of organizations on how the pandemic programs could be more accessible and impactful, and at this time politics seemed to take a break, as so many people really saw that we were in this together. This resulted in significant legislative teamwork by leaders such as Senators Tim Scott, Cory Booker, and Mark Warner, leading to bills that were written but did not ultimately pass, that set forth policy items such as making the U.S. Department of Commerce's Minority Business Development Agency permanent (an action that was ultimately signed into law by President Joe Biden). Much of this work was done with the direct engagement of President Trump's cabinet through the White House Opportunity and Revitalization Council (WHORC). Pursuant to an executive order by President Trump, this committee was made up of almost the entire cabinet and focused exclusively on ways to coordinate agency leadership to maximize dollars and programming for underserved communities. It ensured that these conversations would be not only consistent but intentional, allowing for efficiency and maximum impact, and a model that will be discussed later in greater detail.

During this period, Chris and Ja'Ron became some of the most vocal advocates in the White House for underserved communities. They attended these cabinet-level meetings to put forth programming ideas to account for these groups among the incalculable number of priorities that the COVID pandemic presented. Internal disagreements over funding bills were a daily occurrence, as some saw the circumstances of the pandemic as an all-in situation, whereas others sought to echo playbook conservatism—concerned about what impact new money could have on the long-term economy and the politics of the day. Ultimately—to a certain extent—the latter group won, but there was a wrinkle. The issue was over new money. But what about old money? In a meeting with some of the most important decision-makers on the budget, Ja'Ron and Chris were able to get a commitment that they would consider plans for funds that already had been appropriated. This commitment was the only daylight they needed.

Chris and Ja'Ron spent weeks working with an incredibly committed OMB staff, poring over every existing program—including programs from past administrations that had committed dollars that had not been spent and were just sitting there, having no positive impact on the American people. Not too dissimilar to the plot of the Ivan Reitman–directed film *Dave*, in which a presidential stand-in played by Kevin Kline is seemingly given a fool's errand of finding funds to save a homeless shelter, Chris and Ja'Ron took the opportunity and ran with it. And not only did they make headway in the administration's decision to set aside PPP funding for CDFIs and MDIs, but defunct programs and unappropriated dollars were discovered. If harnessed correctly, this money could have a massive impact on economic development. This will be discussed later in detail, but the effort to find old programs with unspent funds also was a significant part of what would become the Platinum Plan.

Once again, the guideposts of commitment and intentionality were critical to achieving results for underserved communities. The truth is that these policy wins did not come easily. Though commitment and intentionality were the foundation, that alone did not move the needle. For each issue area, Chris and Ja'Ron had to build trust. Building trust and developing collaboration—across the White House, the cabinet agencies, the mayors, and the private sector organizations—allowed them to have honest conversations on what could and could not be achieved. For actions regarding institutions and programs such as HBCUs, OZs, the WHORC, or the PPP, those in the Trump administration had to listen and learn what the stakeholders needed. Once they were committed to addressing those needs, then Chris and Ja'Ron could build trust through listening and learning.

Next, Chris and Ja'Ron had to collaborate—with universities, trade associations, members of Congress, and nonprofits as well as so many other stakeholders on both sides of the aisle—to achieve the policy wins. Finally, by focusing on specific outcomes—such as HBCU funding permanency, OZ impact, or the PPP—they were able to articulate a clear destination and goal. To paraphrase the famous line from *Alice in Wonderland*, if you don't know where you are going, any road will get you there. One of the next roads to be discussed would lead to the passage of historic criminal justice reform legislation: the First Step Act.

CHAPTER **SIX**

Criminal Justice Reform and the Trump Administration's Response: The First Step Act

The end of the Civil War brought about a new kind of racism. The horrible nature of slavery provided a dynamic of property and owner; and now, while technical ownership no longer existed, racism was written into the laws and carried out through their execution. In her book *The New Jim Crow*, Michelle Alexander points out that slavery itself became a legal punishment, citing a case brought to the Virginia Supreme Court (*Ruffin v. Commonwealth*) in which the defendant was sentenced to servitude even though the court stated that he did retain "all his personal rights except those which the law in its humanity accords him."[296] The court went on to bluntly say, "He is for the time being a slave of the State. He is civiliter mortus; and his estate, if he has any, is administered like that of a dead man."[297] Alexander goes on to point out that this

---

[296] Michelle Alexander, *The New Jim Crow: Mass Incarceration in the Age of Colorblindness* (The New Press, 2020), 39.

[297] Alexander, *The New Jim Crow*, 39.

type of thinking led to a prison boom in Mississippi, where "prisoners became younger and blacker, and the length of their sentences soared." She cites the fact that the prison population grew at ten times the rate of the general population.[298]

In states all across the country, the Black inmate population sky-rocketed after the war, as an oft-missed component of the Thirteenth Amendment, which codifies the freedom of former slaves, is an exception for those convicted criminally.[299] Take, for example, the concept of convict leasing, by which a minor infraction could result in a person being rented out to another person or corporation to do work. Using the criminal justice system to meet some of the labor needs of plantation owners and others became a popular practice.[300] The Fourteenth Amendment, which provides birthright citizenship and equal protection for all citizens, has exceptions for convicts as well—namely voting limitations.[301] This incentivized Southerners to convict Black people who they knew would support the Republican agenda, which was abolitionist and pro-Reconstruction. [302]

Over the continuing decades, Black Americans and other minorities experienced increased interactions with the criminal justice system, including arrests.[303] In fact, the Department of Justice published a report saying that from the mid-1920s to the mid-1980s, the percentage of Black

---

[298] Alexander, *The New Jim Crow*, 39.

[299] Section 1 of the Thirteenth Amendment states: "*Neither slavery nor involuntary servitude, except as a punishment for crime whereof the party shall have been duly convicted, shall exist within the United States, or any place subject to their jurisdiction.*" Heather Ann Thompson, "The Racial History of Criminal Justice in America," *Du Bois Review: Social Science Research on Race* 16, no. 1 (2019): 221–41.

[300] Thompson, "The Racial History of Criminal Justice in America."

[301] Thompson, "The Racial History of Criminal Justice in America."

[302] Thompson, "The Racial History of Criminal Justice in America."

[303] Thompson, "The Racial History of Criminal Justice in America."

people in federal penitentiaries doubled to 44 percent. The increase of Black people, along with other minorities, in penitentiaries occurred all across the country—in both the North and the South—due to local laws and ordinances on loitering and being in after-hours bars that were viewed as "Black spaces."[304] Hate strikes by Whites against Blacks happened in major cities such as Detroit and Philadelphia when Black people tried to move into certain neighborhoods, and the offenders were rarely incarcerated for their violent actions.[305] After World War II, reports of mistreatment of Black people by police became much more frequent. This mistreatment included physical assaults accompanied by racial epithets, with 90 percent of those reports coming from Black people with no previous criminal record.[306] This behavior extended from the streets into the prison system itself; reports even shared details of egregious medical experimentation on Black inmates in a prison in Bridgewater, Massachusetts.[307]

The 1960s ushered in a period of both violence and passive resistance, during which Black people and other minorities protested their treatment by the criminal justice and prison systems. Riots occurred within prisons like Attica Correctional Facility in New York; these riots sought in part to bring attention to and remedy the treatment of Black inmates, as the system of discrimination could not be seen by civil society.[308] Even White inmates acknowledged this discrimination, as demonstrated by the fact that one of the Attica prisoners' key demands during the riot was providing education to existing prison personnel and developing a minority hiring program for new corrections officers.[309]

---

[304] Thompson, "The Racial History of Criminal Justice in America."
[305] Thompson, "The Racial History of Criminal Justice in America."
[306] Thompson, "The Racial History of Criminal Justice in America."
[307] Thompson, "The Racial History of Criminal Justice in America."
[308] Thompson, "The Racial History of Criminal Justice in America."
[309] Thompson, "The Racial History of Criminal Justice in America."

As these riots were occurring in the prisons, more aggressive policing of minorities was developing on the streets, coupled with higher rates of incarceration of minorities. This increase led to calls for law and order, which in turn led to additional state laws as well as the Law Enforcement Assistance Act of 1965 (LEAA). President Lyndon Johnson promoted the LEAA, which provided more significant financial support and resources to the law enforcement community and was included in the president's War on Crime announcement that same year.[310]

Over the next decade, additional crime bills were passed with harsher sentences—excessively impacting poor urban people, who were dispro-portionately Black. Critics see these bills as being political, and have shared that certain statistics may have been manipulated to allow de-partments to obtain more LEAA funding based on criminal activity.[311] Critics have also shared that the 1965 LEAA aligned with the passage of the 1964 Civil Rights Act, which potentially provided a way for law-and-order politicians to ensure substantive law enforcement funding would be available even in the midst of historic social reforms.[312] The evidence also demonstrates that rates of incarceration rose in places where education and social services programs were stalled or underfunded, potentially further demonstrating the link between a lack of certain programs and concentrated crime. This cycle continued into the 1970s as manufactur-ing jobs went away and inner-city Black residents had fewer and fewer employment options. [313]

After President Lyndon Johnson's tenure, President Richard Nixon turned the War on Crime into a War on Drugs, which continued into the 1980s, leading to an increased focus on drug-possession arrests during the rise of the crack cocaine era. This led to significant abuse and violence

---

[310] Thompson, "The Racial History of Criminal Justice in America."
[311] Thompson, "The Racial History of Criminal Justice in America."
[312] Thompson, "The Racial History of Criminal Justice in America."
[313] Thompson, "The Racial History of Criminal Justice in America."

in urban areas, as well as severe sentencing penalties. [314] In the 1980s, for example, Black juveniles were transferred to adult courts 37 percent more often than other populations, and Black people were more likely to receive longer prison sentences than Whites.[315] Bolstered by the 1984 Comprehensive Crime Control Act, which eliminated federal parole, and the 1986 Anti-Drug Abuse Act, which provided mandatory minimum sentencing requirements, the era of crack cocaine became known for its harsh sentencing for crack possession and dealing; and although their chemical makeup was consistent, significant disparities in sentencing occurred for offenses involving crack versus powder cocaine.[316]

The 1990s saw increased penalties and additional mandatory minimum sentencing with the advent of the Violent Crime Control and Law Enforcement Act of 1994, and poor minorities often had to plea-bargain. President Bill Clinton, famous for saying during his first presidential campaign in 1992 that he "didn't inhale" any marijuana smoke while experimenting with the drug as a student in England, also said that he would be tougher on crime than any of his Republican opponents. He went on to support the Violent Crime Control and Law Enforcement Act in his 1994 State of the Union address.[317]

The act would lead to the largest prison population in history, as well as higher levels of capital cases.[318] It expanded the death penalty on a historic level, impacted legal standards of habeas corpus, permitted the trying of thirteen-year-olds as adults, eliminated Pell Grants for prisoners, extended the three-strikes law, and included various state incentives

---

[314] Alexander, *The New Jim Crow*, 67.
[315] Alexander, *The New Jim Crow*, 67.
[316] Alexander, *The New Jim Crow*, 68.
[317] William Clinton, 1994 Presidential State of the Union address, January 25, 1994, https://www.presidency.ucsb.edu/documents/address-before-joint-session-the-congress-the-state-the-union-12.
[318] Alexander, *The New Jim Crow*, 67–68.

to promote a tough-on-crime approach. By 2010, most federal inmates were incarcerated for drug offenses—fewer than 10 percent of them had committed violence.[319]

But potentially most disturbing about all of this is the negative impact that prison itself had as a reform mechanism. The increase in law enforcement budgets coincided with increases in jail populations and the associated prison construction.[320] The new mandatory minimum sentences contributed significantly to increasing rates of recidivism, partly because time inside prison can become something of a criminal school that establishes an internal and external network that often promotes the vicious criminal cycle. The sheer numbers of individuals going through the criminal justice system exacerbated this reality; and in many cases, it was the families of the convicts that were severely impacted, as financial and parental stability is decimated—which can of course lead to illegal activity by the next generation.[321]

Growing up in the 1980s and 1990s, Ja'Ron was exposed to criminal behavior in his neighborhood, but one of the great blessings of his life is that he had a strong father who helped him to navigate his community. In fact, his father had gotten involved in selling and using drugs in the 1960s, '70s, and '80s; but by the time Ja'Ron was born, his father had left that life behind. That said, Ja'Ron's father was able to draw on those

---

[319] Thompson, "The Racial History of Criminal Justice in America."

[320] Alexander, *The New Jim Crow*, 71.

[321] *"Finally, while changes in criminal law, sentencing policy, policing, and prosecutorial practices all help to explain today's high rate of incarceration as well as why that rate is so racially skewed, ironically, today's high rate of incarceration itself is also a factor. Prisons are criminogenic. Not only are they schools of crime, they also destroy the social fabric of families and communities… Because of mass incarceration's scale and impact on poor communities of color, the children of incarcerated adults experience greater poverty as well as increased anti-social behavior and illegal activity. The results are higher rates of policing, more incarceration, more poverty, and so on."* Thompson, "The Racial History of Criminal Justice in America," 14.

experiences and share them with his son, and he successfully protected Ja'Ron from going down that same road. While Ja'Ron's father never went to prison, the criminal behavior of many of his father's friends led to their imprisonment or death.

Ja'Ron admittedly had brushes with the law when he was younger, but unfortunately, he has also had friends who went to prison or lost their lives at the hands of gang violence. Ja'Ron's experience with the criminal justice system did not result in a criminal record, but the cost of criminal defense took a significant toll—setting him back almost a decade financially. He recalls being arrested in a majority-White suburb of Cleveland, Ohio. He was shocked that almost all of the defendants in the courthouse were Black—and the only White people in the courtroom were the police, bailiffs, and the judge. He also saw firsthand that the public defenders were overwhelmed with cases, and that many of the defendants were faced with little choice other than to accept plea bargains; otherwise, they would have risked much larger sentences at trial.

After his legal troubles, Ja'Ron turned to alcohol and almost lost his job. It was about that time that he became very active in his church. His engagement as a mentor in the church's jobs partnership program, along with personal therapy, was transformational for him. In this new role, he mentored many former inmates, and he recognized that his life's purpose was one of service. He recalls praying to God, promising that if he survived hitting rock bottom, he would commit himself to others. It was this experience that would lead him back into the classroom—at Howard University's School of Divinity in Washington, D.C.

Ja'Ron gave himself one year to pay back the debt he owed to those who had paid his legal expenses, and without a job or any prospects, he moved out of Cleveland back to the Howard University campus. He distinctly remembers packing up all of his belongings in his car, putting his hands on the steering wheel, and acknowledging that his life was all in God's hands. Upon landing back in the nation's capital, Ja'Ron got a job on Capitol Hill working for a then congressman and future vice president—Mike Pence, where he began to learn how to navigate Congress. After graduating the Howard Divinity program, Ja'Ron would put this skill to work alongside President Trump in a generational criminal justice reform bill known as the First Step Act. Keeping to his personal commitment after his own experience, he saw this as an opportunity to make the system fairer and to generate opportunities for those who had paid their debt to society.

The First Step Act is a perfect example of the importance of intentionality in building a policy portfolio. Formally known as the Formerly Incarcerated Reenter Society Transformed Safely Transitioning Every Person Act, it began as a bipartisan criminal justice bill—the first of its kind in over twenty years. It focuses on federal prison reform, a reduction in recidivism, and public safety and workforce opportunities, among other important areas. The basic premise of the act, which was signed into law in 2018, is that lower recidivism rates contribute to safer communities, and more safety leads to more economic investment in those communities. It was championed by Presidential Advisor Jared Kushner, as outlined in his book, *Breaking History*, and was shepherded through the legislative process in large part by Ja'Ron.

The First Step Act is an excellent illustration of what can be achieved when elected officials get together and identify a population that needs help, then find a way to help. Like any legislation, it is the product of compromise and struggle, but its enactment has led to the release of nonviolent felons who have done their time, and has provided a pathway to minimize the chances of their once-likely return to prison. While the act was bipartisan from a political perspective, even notable pundits on the left—such as Van Jones and Jessica Jackson, cofounders of the #Cut50 initiative—were engaged, given its uniqueness.[322] As Jones has stated,

---

[322] *"#cut50 represents the idea that we can cut the prison population and crime in 50 percent in the next 10 years by, instead of employing tough on crime policies,*

"For some, it's hard to imagine anything good happening in the middle of the Trump era—especially for Black, brown, and low-income people. But believe it or not, something truly beautiful is happening in Washington, D.C, on the least likely of issues—criminal justice reform."[323]

Not only was it a difficult process, but it was a fight that did not initially seem to be one in which the administration was going to engage. The administration had so many priorities in its early days, and the underserved community of the incarcerated and formerly incarcerated is too often one that gets overlooked. Of course, at the end of any administration, presidents often pardon imprisoned or formerly imprisoned individuals who have demonstrated some level of rehabilitation, but to fully engage and use political capital to benefit a community that is too often at the boundaries of civil society is typically not a priority for either side of the aisle. The concept of a fair criminal justice system might be discussed in sound bites, but for conservatives to truly take this fight to Capitol Hill was more or less unheard of. In this case, however, they did take on the fight, and with an intentional approach. The effort began with a very small team. In fact, as Steve Smith, the chief of staff for the Office of American Innovation recalls, the first meeting on the First Step Act concept was scheduled for the War Department Secretary's Room—one of the grand meeting spaces of the Eisenhower Executive Office Building. However, due to low attendance, it was moved to a much smaller room.[324]

But a slow start did not stop the committed team. The next step was coalition building. This effort at first was very small and very slow. People

---

employing smart safety solutions. I co-founded #cut50 with Van Jones and Matt Haney. I chose to come on board because I believe it's time for transformative change as opposed to just incremental change, and I really wanted to reduce the stigma." Camille Augustin, "#Cut50 Co-Founder Jessica Jackson Sloan Breaks Down the Mechanics of Mass Incarceration," *Vibe*, December 29, 2017, https://www.vibe.com/features/editorial/jessica-jackson-cut50-meek-mill-interview-553078/.

[323] Interview with Jessica Jackson, August 2022.

[324] Interview with Steve Smith, September 2022.

such as criminal justice advocate Doug Deason and organizations such as the Koch Network, Safe Streets and Second Chances, The Heritage Foundation, and Right on Crime, an organization under the Texas Public Policy Foundation (TPPF), became important leaders in this effort. In fact, TPPF's then president, Brooke Rollins, became integral to this effort and eventually many other policy initiatives in the Trump White House.

Rollins came to the White House as an invitee to the coalition that Jared Kushner was developing for this effort. Her experience working as counsel to Texas Governor Rick Perry and her successes in criminal justice reform in that state made her an ideal person to help lead this effort at the federal level. Given her talent and passion, she essentially walked in a guest and walked out a White House employee in the Office of American Innovation. Soon the handful of organizations involved grew to nearly five hundred and represented the full spectrum of conservative and liberal political ideologies—but with the common goal of advancing criminal justice reform. The coalition meetings to develop a legislative strategy went from monthly to weekly to daily, and none of the discussions were ever leaked—a unique situation to which any experienced Washington professional can attest. Remembering these special circumstances and the commitment of everyone around the table, Steve Smith accounts for this D.C. rarity by noting that the group "established trust through trials."[325]

The most prominent left-leaning group at the table was #Cut50, an initiative headed by pundit and activist Van Jones and Jessica Jackson. While Jackson may not be a household name, she is one of the most impactful advocates for criminal justice reform in the country. An attorney and former mayor in California, she has worked with some of the largest names in media and entertainment to advance the cause—and suffice it to say that she is not a Republican. Among other roles that Jackson maintains, she served as Kim Kardashian's mentor in her legal

---

[325] Interview with Steve Smith, September 2022.

apprenticeship—which is a requirement to sit for the California bar exam. As the child of a criminal defense attorney, Robert Kardashian, the younger Kardashian was just as committed to seeing this legislation pass as everyone else on the team. She became an important advocate for the passage and implementation of the First Step Act and the pardon of former federal prisoner Alice Johnson, among others.[326]

Jones and Jackson had been fighting for this kind of change for quite some time and were no strangers to working across the aisle to advance the cause. A few years earlier, they had arranged a summit with former Speaker Newt Gingrich, the Koch organization, and the American Civil Liberties Union to discuss the issue.[327] Jackson recalls that at this time, Jones received a call saying that Jared Kushner wanted to speak with him.[328] They didn't know each other, but Jones had been informed that Kushner was serious about having a conversation on criminal justice reform.[329] Recognizing that while the optics of such a meeting might not be great, but also thinking—as Jackson shares about Jones—that his worst

---

[326] *"Alice Johnson, a woman who had been sentenced to life in prison for a nonviolent drug offense, praised President Trump at the Republican National Convention Thursday for commuting her sentence and signing the bipartisan criminal justice reform First Step Act. 'I was once told that the only way I would ever be reunited with my family would be as a corpse,' Johnson said. 'But by the grace of God and the compassion of President Donald John Trump, I stand before you tonight…and I assure you, I'm not a ghost. I am alive, I am well, and most importantly, I am free.' Trump commuted Johnson's sentence in 2018 at the urging of Kim Kardashian-West, a justice reform advocate. 'Some say, 'You do the crime. You do the time.' However, that time should be fair and just,' Johnson said. 'We've all made mistakes, and none of us want to be defined forever based on our worst decision.'"* Zack Budryk, "Alice Johnson Praises Trump for First Step Act, Urges Compassion for 'Forgotten Faces,'" The Hill, August 27, 2020, https://thehill.com/homenews/campaign/514085-alice-johnson-praises-trump-for-first-step-act-urges-compassion-for/.

[327] Interview with Jessica Jackson, August 2022.

[328] Interview with Jessica Jackson, August 2022.

[329] Interview with Jessica Jackson, August 2022.

day on Twitter would be better than someone's best day in prison, Jones took a chance on the meeting.[330] According to Jackson, in that meeting, Kushner spoke of his own father's incarceration and the impact that it had on him and his family.[331] The attendees walked out of that meeting noting Kushner's sincerity and thinking that his offer to work together was genuine.[332] While other well-known groups on the left chose to sit out the early days of this effort, the #Cut50 team became very engaged. And as Jackson puts it, the more she and the others worked with Kushner, the stronger their trust in him became. She says that every time the team conveyed that an approach or a clause "was not okay, Jared went to bat for them."[333]

One of the next steps in the process of developing the First Step Act was to set up meetings for President Trump so he could get comfortable with the group's propositions. While he had campaigned on being the president for forgotten communities, this was one the first true tests of that promise. Those meetings included sit-downs with governors who had guided successful criminal justice reform efforts in their states, led by the Texas example of former Governor Perry, who had overseen the closure of ten prisons and almost all of Texas' juvenile facilities under his state's reforms.

Trump also met with faith leaders and other key advisory groups, but he wanted to ensure that whatever legislation was passed had the support of the law enforcement community. After many conversations with key law enforcement constituencies and the development of a presidential commission to study police modernization, all of the constituencies agreed with the legislation.

---

[330] Interview with Jessica Jackson, August 2022.
[331] Interview with Jessica Jackson, August 2022.
[332] Interview with Jessica Jackson, August 2022.
[333] Interview with Jessica Jackson, August 2022.

Now it needed to get through Congress. Initial meetings with congressional leadership in 2018 pointed to the fact that the legislation might get pushed to the so-called lame-duck session—the time after an election but before the new Congress is sworn in. In Washington, a bill getting pushed to this time is tantamount to killing the bill. To achieve its goal, the White House team met with every Republican senator. Jones and Jackson were confident that they could get the Democrats, and celebrities including Kim Kardashian expertly used their social media platforms to keep the bill in the pop culture zeitgeist. The team "stayed on offense," as Brooke Rollins likes to say, and the bill passed in December 2018.

As discussed earlier, this story has protagonists and antagonists. And ironically, this disagreement came from the inside. You see, *criminal justice reform* means a lot of things to a lot of people, and it is often portrayed as being soft on crime. Passing mandatory minimums for sentencing, for example, typically translates into being tough on crime in a political stump speech, but the practical impact may be the recidivism that society hopes to avoid. Many of the nonviolent offenders within the scope of this legislation are born into a system that depends upon government programs. With little incentive and few role models for advancement, these people often depend on petty crimes simply for survival, which can lead to drug use and possession. Without the tools to break that cycle during prison time, they almost inevitably end up back in prison. And while incarceration certainly is appropriate for some, there are countless individuals who have paid their debt to society and need a real chance to learn to be productive.

The First Step Act provides for that chance, but the monolithic tough-on-crime mentality of certain members of the Republican party made the act's passage an uphill battle. That battle became compounded by large well-known liberal organizations lobbying congressional members not to support this plan, due to that fact that it originated from the Trump White House.

But then there were the protagonists, and they were not necessarily who you might think they were. Republican politicians such as Senator Ted Cruz and Representative Jim Jordan came together with Democrats such as Senator Dick Durbin and Representative Hakeem Jeffries to advance the bill. While many high-profile Democrats either openly opposed the bill or did little to advance it, and while even groups such as the Congressional Black Caucus were split, champions like Cruz, Durbin, Jeffries, and Jordan worked tirelessly across the aisle to get this first criminal justice reform bill in almost twenty-five years completed.

The leaders of the national police unions and organizations—including the Fraternal Order of Police—were also critical to the legislation's success. Law enforcement was a strong political base for President Trump, and its leaders needed to be in the room to get the bill signed into law. Their commitment, cooperation, and candor allowed for a real discussion with political leaders and liberal community groups, all of which were critical to advancing this reform. And the trust that grew became the basis for work that would be done just a couple of years later, in the summer of 2020, when Congress was unable to provide a legislative solution to policing reform.

Along with Kushner, Jones, Jackson, and congressional leaders, Ja'Ron stood over President Trump's shoulder as he signed the First Step Act into law. Once he had finished, Trump congratulated Ja'Ron for his ability to coordinate a bipartisan accomplishment. And, as often happens in government and corporate America, once a talent is recognized, the person is asked to engage in the next challenge. That same day, due to an inability of Congress and the White House to resolve a spending bill, the U.S. government underwent its longest shutdown in history, and Ja'Ron was asked to apply his talents to a bipartisan solution for reopening—but that is a different story for a different day.

Once the First Step Act became law, the cabinet agencies all leaned into fostering its impact. For example, at the Small Business Administration,

Chris initiated regional conferences in part to promote second-chance hiring of the formerly incarcerated by small and medium-size businesses. By highlighting these hiring opportunities for these businesses and show-casing how large companies such as JPMorgan Chase and groups such as the Business Roundtable's Second Chance Business Coalition had been successful on this path, he and the organizers sought to provide these smaller companies with an approach they could duplicate for their hiring needs.[334]

In fact, at one such conference, Chris met the leaders of the Pivot Program at Georgetown University—an entrepreneurial support program

---

[334] We Advance Second Chances (Second Chance Business Coalition: *"An enduring belief in the American dream has powered decades of innovation, inspired genera-tions of entrepreneurs and driven the economic growth of our nation. But that dream is fraying for the nearly one in three U.S. adults – or 78 million Americans – who have a criminal record. For many of these individuals, a criminal record poses a significant barrier to employment, even when the record includes only a misde-meanor arrest or conviction. Regardless of their qualifications, these individuals struggle to participate in the American workforce and contribute to their families and society. And there's an opportunity cost for employers as well, who are unable to benefit from the talents of tens of millions of qualified candidates. When people are given a fair opportunity to participate in the workforce, our economy and society are stronger. That is why we're proud to serve as co-chairs of the Second Chance Business Coalition. Our goal is to encourage the nation's largest employers to give more people with criminal backgrounds a second chance at the dignity of a good job and a better life for themselves and their families. More inclusive hiring is a powerful way to break the cycle of poverty in many American communities. Having a fair opportu-nity for employment helps individuals and families strengthen their financial health and give back to their communities. These improvements translate to a better local economy, which boosts the business climate for all companies. The Second Chance Business Coalition is a powerful effort to fortify the American dream and give many in our society a second chance they otherwise might never have."* From Chairs Jamie Dimon (CEO—JP Morgan Chase) and Craig Arnold (CEO—Eaton), Second Chance Business Coalition, https://secondchancebusinesscoalition.org/about.

for the formerly incarcerated.[335] He invited all of the program participants to the SBA to learn from all of the small business program offices. Ja'Ron joined Chris at that event and spoke to them about the importance of the First Step Act and the process of getting it passed. Chris recalls speaking with the director of the Pivot Program before the visit, saying that while the agency employees and information they could share were fantastic, the SBA was just a typical, somewhat bland government building. The Pivot Program director responded that being invited into a government building whose staff would seek to help them was very much a welcomed experience, as so many of them associated time in government buildings with their time spent in prison and other areas of the criminal justice

---

[335] *"The Georgetown University Pivot Program is a business and entrepreneurship-oriented reentry program, delivered by Georgetown University in partnership with the D.C. Department of Employment Services. The program, which combines classroom training with subsidized internships at local businesses and non-profits, is designed to change the attitude of employers toward the hiring of individuals with prior criminal convictions, and to allow returning citizens to access opportunities that would be otherwise out of reach. We also hope that Pivot Program graduates will create jobs for themselves and for others through business enterprises of their own. Across the United States, more than seven million Americans currently are under some form of correctional control – including incarceration, parole, and probation – and one in three adults has a criminal record. In the District of Columbia alone, as many as 5,000 individuals are released from prison or jail every year, and less than half of them find sustainable employment. This perpetuates a cycle of crime and incarceration, with devastating effects on families, communities, and the broader economy. The Pivot Program seeks to break that cycle and recognize this untapped human capital by supporting a set of people who have previously made mistakes, served their time, and are committed to becoming successful leaders and role models in their communities. Our approach is based on the premise that a combination of higher education and employment – together with the social, emotional, and intellectual development that takes place in a university environment – will succeed in preparing returning citizens for positions as both entrepreneurial leaders or productive employees. The Pivot Program represents a collaboration between Georgetown's Prisons and Justice Initiative, the McDonough School of Business and Georgetown College with substantial support from the D.C. Department of Employment Services."* "About," Pivot Program, Georgetown University, https://pivot.georgetown.edu/about/.

system. Once again, Chris appreciated the lessons from his college professor and the importance of putting oneself in another person's shoes when developing policy approaches.

Achieving such landmark legislation as the First Step Act in a bipartisan fashion is very unique in today's political environment. There is a historical sense that politicians have always achieved their landmark legislation in smoke-filled back rooms, or through intimidation such as President Lyndon Johnson's famous in-your-face arm-twisting, but Jessica Jackson conveys a much more fascinating approach. "To me, to reach bipartisan legislation, you have to start with humanizing the issue," she says.[336] She recalls that in the early days of the First Step Act, stories of pregnant women being shackled, of loved ones left behind by the incarcerated, and many other heartbreaking accounts elevated the voices of those impacted by the criminal justice system "and opened up the heart space," so that policy makers on both sides of the aisle could understand that real people would be greatly affected by the legislation.[337] In fact, Jackson believes that one of the biggest mistakes that people can make is not accounting for the experiences of others. She expresses that her work in criminal justice reform is informed by her time as a defense attorney and a family member of an incarcerated individual. She is quick to point out that her lens is limited in scope, as she has not been a victim of a crime, nor has she been a police officer who witnessed or responded to a crime, or a paramedic or a member of a community impacted by criminal behavior.[338] That said, walking through those other perspectives is where she seeks to begin the process of accounting for the experiences of others.[339] Those relationships and that trust—particularly as developed

---

[336] Interview with Jessica Jackson, August 2022.
[337] Interview with Jessica Jackson, August 2022.
[338] Interview with Jessica Jackson, August 2022.
[339] Interview with Jessica Jackson, August 2022.

with Jessica and the law enforcement groups—would become critical just eighteen months later in the summer of 2020.

After the death of George Floyd in the summer of 2020, police reform became the most politically charged issue facing America, and ultrapartisanship blinded elected leaders so they could not recognize and collectively advance plans that would benefit our citizenry. With Congress unable to come to an agreement on police reform legislation, Ja'Ron and Chris worked night and day under Jared Kushner's leadership on the development of an executive order that would address the country's needs but also be implementable. Working alongside Attorney General Bill Barr, the White House Counsel's Office, and other senior White House staff, Chris and Ja'Ron engaged directly with many of the community activists and senior law enforcement groups that had been involved with passage of the First Step Act to reach an impactful consensus. Getting an executive order drafted is very different from getting legislation passed, but the entire text of the final executive order passed through the lens of those trusted partners at a critical time in our American history.

President Trump's approach to criminal justice reform was always to support law enforcement so that more crime could be prevented and more communities could be considered for economic investment. It became a necessity to take action, however, because of the riots, lawlessness, and frankly the feeling that the streets were a tinderbox just waiting for a match. Despite his best efforts, Senator Tim Scott was unable to get bipartisan consensus for a sober legislative solution to address these issues of policing, while certain liberal officials proposed bills that they knew would not pass. Political approaches like this may have their place, but there is no time when the art of legislative leadership is more important than in a crisis, and many saw this as a political moment for an election just a few months away. But facing the reality of looting, massive property damage, civil unrest, and calls to defund the police that summer, action needed to happen. So Jared, Ja'Ron, Chris, their colleague Jack

Rauch, and the rest of the administration team gathered some of the same coalition from the First Step Act—including Jessica Jackson and the police unions. They worked continuously, sharing confidential drafts of the executive order back and forth—with countless calls in between, exhibiting the same trust as during the process of passing the First Step Act. In fact, in the midst of their literal typing, Chris and Ja'Ron observed that the cable news media outlets were sharing information about the order's supposed contents. The media reports often entirely missed the mark, citing sources that had no fingerprints on the actual contents of the executive order or the intention behind what was being written.

With around-the-clock work and coordination, the executive order was completed, and the associated signing ceremony was consistent with many of the public White House activities to which the American public has grown accustomed. Ja'Ron and Chris stood at the front of the audience in the Rose Garden between the attorney general and the acting secretary of the Department of Homeland Security, while President Trump signed the executive order amid several uniformed police officials. But almost more important was what had happened just a few minutes earlier.

A little backstory: The call for police reform had boiled over with George Floyd, but many other individuals had become synonymous with it—people such as Ahmaud Arbery and Breonna Taylor, both of whom had lost their lives in circumstances enveloped in allegations of racist behavior by citizens and the police. Many of those individuals' families were represented by an attorney named Lee Merritt. Just before the signing of the executive order, many of those families and Mr. Merritt met with President Trump and Attorney General Barr in the East Room of the White House.

Approximately forty people were present, including Chris and Ja'Ron. President Trump asked each family to speak, and each provided a firsthand account of their loss and the impact on their family and their community. It was the kind of event that many presidents do in public.

But there were no cameras; there were no press microphones. It was an honest conversation between this devastated community of people and their president. And while it seemed unlikely that any of them had voted or were going to vote for Trump, frankly that did not matter, as he and the attorney general made solemn commitments to them away from the cameras. None of these individuals joined in the Rose Garden event, but that in no way took away from the work that the Department of Justice would continue to do on these issues. And it is important to note that the Department of Justice played a critical role in the creation of this executive order—including overseeing the training and accreditation of police departments on lethal force, as well as working with the Department of Health and Human Services on mental health support and on the engagement of social workers when apprehending homeless, addicted, and other nonviolent offenders.

When Jessica Jackson was asked by the authors of this book as to what struck her about all of her work with President Trump, she responded that he seemed to take a very sincere approach to the issue of criminal justice reform.[340] She said that he listened to formerly incarcerated people that she had brought to the White House; he listened to their families; and over the many months during which this legislation was developed, he remembered details that were personal—not political, and certainly not for the cameras.[341] She recalls that in the meeting with the families of the victims, some of whom had died at the hands of police officers, he just listened; and when the families were done speaking, he immediately asked Attorney General Barr to look into the status of the matters.[342] And in line with the concepts of intentionality and collaboration, sure enough, Barr contacted Jackson the very next day to talk about these cases.[343]

---

340 Interview with Jessica Jackson, August 2022.
341 Interview with Jessica Jackson, August 2022.
342 Interview with Jessica Jackson, August 2022.
343 Interview with Jessica Jackson, August 2022.

And as is typical for the parlor games of Washington, despite the Democrats' criticism of Trump's executive order, the Biden administration came out with ostensibly a carbon-copy version of it almost two years later. For purposes of comparison, Trump's executive order set forth provisions for certification and independent credentialing for police departments on use-of-force standards; national information sharing on excessive force incidents; prohibition on the use of chokeholds except as allowed by law; access to training and technical assistance on use-of-force matters for police departments, including de-escalation techniques; social worker support for the mentally ill, homeless, and addicted; community outreach programs; and officer mental health and wellness programs. Once in place, Trump's executive order resulted in thousands more police departments being accredited in use-of-force standards than at any time in the past. The Biden administration's executive order adopted much of the same language and concepts, and even went so far as to call for the full implementation of the Trump administration's First Step Act.

Thinking back to the summer of 2020—the tanks surrounding Washington, the violence in the streets and in communities—Chris and Ja'Ron feel that their most disappointing memory is the inability for elected officials to come to the table and resolve through legislation something that America needed to solve in real time. It may seem like editorializing, but it is worth noting that while Congress could not come to a vote on anything around police reform in the midst of everything that occurred in that summer, this executive order was the only action that a president could take, and the engaged community activist and law enforcement groups agreed on almost 90 percent of its contents. Instead of inspiring his party's members to advance a legislative solution in real time, the Democratic Senate minority leader took to the microphones and simply said that President Trump's executive order would "not deliver comprehensive meaningful change," referring to it simply as "weak tea."[344] However, as of this writing, even with a majority in both the houses of Congress and a Democratic president, this now Senate majority leader has achieved no success delivering the meaningful change on policing reforms that he indicated was absent from Trump's 2020 action.

Most of the work that administrations do is not conducted in front of the camera. And while signing ceremonies and political rallies may be what brings the media out and gets people to tune in, the most important work is meeting with stakeholders and hearing their concerns. It is those intentional and very personal interactions that can bring political foes together to remember why they were elected in the first place. Despite any criticisms that may remain, the First Step Act and Trump's executive order on policing accomplished those interactions. It is good to remember that many actions such as these are simply a start—and that a thousand-mile journey begins with the first step.

---

[344] "Trump to Release Police Reform Proposals That Focus on Training," *Washington Post*, June 16, 2020, https://www.washingtonpost.com/politics/ trump-to-release-police-reform-proposals-that-focus-on-training/2020/06/16/ f41f0eb6-afdb-11ea-8f56-63f38c990077_story.html

CHAPTER **SEVEN**

The Country's Unfinished Business: The White House Opportunity and Revitalization Council and the Platinum Plan

D espite what most people think, conservative economists tend to recognize the need for government action in certain market events. One can look back as recently as the initial economic response to the COVID pandemic as an example of how an elastic approach to capitalism in times of crisis is consistent with a conservative approach to democracy. But the most impactful version of such a response includes: a recognition that a problem exists; a thoughtful and bipartisan approach to addressing the problem; and a sustained approach that is intentional, consistently measured, and able to continue without political frailty. So when it comes to underserved communities, let us take a representative view of what conservative economists might say in response to the market failure facing them, through the lens of Milton Friedman, who famously stated that "one of the great mistakes is to judge policies and programs by their intentions rather than their results," and that "nothing is so permanent as a temporary government program."[345]

Based on the above, it is clear that Friedman would have supported a free-market approach to advance underserved communities, one that that would be results-oriented, truly temporary, and beneficial for all parties. The authors contend that Thomas Sowell would concur with this. In his unique style, he made the clear case that the private sector plays a critical role in addressing this issue when he said:

> *It was Thomas Edison who brought us electricity, not the Sierra Club. It was the Wright brothers who got us off the ground, not the Federal Aviation Administration. It was Henry Ford who ended the isolation of millions of Americans by making the automobile affordable, not Ralph Nader. Those who have helped the poor the most have not been those who have gone around loudly expressing "compassion" for the poor, but those who found ways to make industry more productive and distribution more efficient, so that the poor of today can afford things that the affluent of yesterday could only dream about.*[346]

As policy professionals, Chris and Ja'Ron had the great privilege of effecting change for underserved communities in the Trump administration. In areas such as criminal justice reform and economic development, they were able to serve as both mechanic and driver in what must be a race to address the plight of underserved communities. And while nothing is perfect, a great deal still remains to be done, as evidenced by the words of Tocqueville when he said, "The great privilege of the Americans does

---

[345] "Milton Friedman Quotes," Goodreads, https://www.goodreads.com/author/quotes/5001.Milton_Friedman.

[346] "Thomas Sowell Quotes."

not simply consist in their being more enlightened than other nations, but in their being able to repair the faults that they may commit." This quote does not speak just to the Judeo-Christian concept of forgiveness and reconciliation, but rather to the idea that as an American people we can evolve from generation to generation. However, that evolution is not always smooth and it is not always predictable; and it only works when it is intentional. That intentional evolution is much of what the Trump administration sought to accomplish for underserved communities.

As director of Urban Affairs at the White House, Ja'Ron worked to build on a policy framework that was rooted in the work of conservative thinkers like Friedman and Sowell. However, he also had to deal with the practical reality of what currently existed at the federal level. The experience that shaped his world view came in part from his time serving for Representative Jim Jordan on the Republican Study Committee—a conservative caucus that has helped to set the legislative and policy standards for the party for the last fifty years. Traditionally, this committee applied a very conservative approach to creating more limited government by cutting domestic spending by eliminating certain unnecessary programs. Those actions often precipitated significant impacts on certain dependent communities, as people reacted to the cancellation of outdated and duplicative programs.

So instead of taking this strict approach toward reforming the current system, upon which underserved communities had grown to rely, Ja'Ron sought to implement a more pragmatic methodology that would allow changes over time. This policy approach set the stage for a transition from an overdependence on the federal government to a return to a more self-sustainable market approach in civil society—a perspective that was embraced by the Trump administration. By incorporating institutional change that included intentionality and measurable impact, notwithstanding political headwinds from both sides of the aisle, the administration established a number of truly foundational achievements.

Any government entity that works within a silo will have significantly less impact than one that implements a process to share information across its ranks in real time. One could theoretically seek to tie sporadic initiatives together, but without the larger vision of how they can combine to serve as a force multiplier, they are likely to remain as simply piecemeal, significantly limiting their impact. But as alluded to throughout this book, experience, relationships, and intentionality can open the door for dedicated funding to advance practical initiatives that promote opportunity as opposed to perpetuating reliance.

Wayne State Associate Professor Kidada Williams has intimated that the reason the former slaves spent so much time debating the meaning of freedom in those years after the Civil War was because no one thinks more about freedom than one who has been denied it.[347] Further, Williams goes on to share that the Black people who had those conversations in the churches and other gathering places were talking not about the Constitution per se, but about the Declaration of Independence—which highlights that "all men are created equal."[348] This is a critical element to the analysis contained within these pages as it relates back to the very foundations of this country. Given Ja'Ron's experience as a Black man, and the authors' collective policy acumen related to underserved communities, it is their intention to weave together experience, academic study, and thousands of conversations with impacted individuals, representative organizations, policy makers, and other stakeholders to provide a restorative model that can and must succeed—just as that Declaration has done since 1776.

The long game for underserved communities involves allowing enough time for them to transition from dependence on the federal

---

[347] "How Ex-Slaves Built New Lives for Themselves—and America—After the Civil War," *History Unplugged Podcast*, March 18, 2021.

[348] "How Ex-Slaves Built New Lives for Themselves—and America—After the Civil War."

government to an infrastructure of opportunity that is more sustainable and focused on outcomes in the private sector and, accordingly, in civil society. This chapter's title references "unfinished business," which of course is an allusion to President Trump's one term in office. However, it is important to note that having an intentional strategy focused on outcomes can help get us to a place where that version of opportunity is a reality. Politics has unfortunately become more important than change for many elected leaders. This is why it is time for the government to provide a committed framework and for the private sector to lead the way. The potential model framework that the Trump administration initiated, the White House Opportunity and Revitalization Council (WHORC), was created by an executive order. It was made up mostly of cabinet secretaries, and served the general purpose of aligning programs and opportunities for America's underserved communities.

The specific charge of the WHORC included assessing and consulting on the actions each agency can take under existing authorities to:

(1) Prioritize or focus federal investments and programs on urban and economically distressed communities, including qualified opportunity zones;

(2) Minimize all regulatory and administrative costs and burdens that discourage public and private investment in urban and economically distressed communities, including qualified opportunity zones;

(3) Engage with officials from state, local, and tribal governments, and individuals from the private sector to solicit feedback on how best to stimulate the economic development of urban and economically distressed areas, including qualified opportunity zones;

(4) Coordinate federal interagency efforts to develop economic growth strategies for private and public stakeholders—such as

investors, business owners, universities; state, local, and tribal leaders; public housing agencies, nonprofit organizations, and economic development organizations;

(5) Reduce and streamline regulatory and administrative burdens, including burdens on applicants applying for multiple federal assistance awards; and

(6) Help community-based applicants identify and apply for relevant federal resources.[349]

In short, the goal for the WHORC was for the private sector and all three levels of government to create a comprehensive strategy to revitalize distressed communities around the country.

One would think that such an organization would not be necessary. Each of these senior government officials works for the president, and whether those staffers number in the thousands, tens of thousands, or hundreds of thousands, they should all row in the same direction. For many policies that is exactly the case, but for the various issues that impact underserved communities, well-intentioned coordination for any administration—Democrat or Republican—can be bureaucratic and challenging. Having the secretaries in the room together and laying out very specific plans, identifying where partnerships can serve as force multipliers, and citing regulatory and budgetary challenges that can be either removed or mitigated by White House action are critical pieces of this vision.

Many excellent programs often operate in a vacuum, but their shared success across the entire executive branch can be a very powerful thing. Not only does it allow the White House to use its advocacy power and convening capabilities, but it gives the agencies the opportunity to be very

---

[349] "The White House Opportunity and Revitalization Council," U.S. Department of Housing and Urban Development, https://opportunityzones.hud.gov/thecouncil.

intentional in grant-funding and utilizing other resources it shares with nonprofit organizations and public-private partnerships. Many mayors depend on a similar model, and given their smaller bases, they often can achieve their goals with greater speed. As such, many of the country's mayors engaged very directly with the WHORC's actions and leaders, inviting cabinet members to listening sessions in order to advance specific initiatives that would lead to jobs and other economic development in their regions. It was the beginning of that Marshall Plan–type effort for underserved communities.

The WHORC was chaired by the Department of Housing and Urban Development Secretary Ben Carson. His lieutenant was Scott Turner—a former NFL player and state legislator from Texas. In his role as director of the WHORC, Scott traveled to eighty cities—many of them more than once—to tour and review plans for opportunity zones.[350] He would then report back to Secretary Carson as well as to the cabinet members who served on the WHORC. He would also report back to President Trump himself—answering many off-camera inquiries from the president about the state of things in the various communities.[351] In fact, Trump even had Scott present at a full cabinet meeting so that the entirety of his leadership team would be well informed about what was and was not working in the underserved communities that Scott visited. Scott saw that the single commonality of all of the towns he visited—urban, rural, or tribal—was the problem of economic poverty.[352] He told the authors that this poverty was not about color or ethnicity, but rather it stemmed from a history of policies that had taken away real opportunities from these areas, many of which were even losing the members of their youngest generation to other locations where they could find work.[353]

---

[350] Interview with Scott Turner, August 2022.
[351] Interview with Scott Turner, August 2022.
[352] Interview with Scott Turner, August 2022.
[353] Interview with Scott Turner, August 2022

Scott shares that he has kept in touch with many people and has seen that much of the initial work the WHORC team did is now beginning to bear fruit; and when he was asked where that work will go from here, he simply indicated that this work should be picked up exactly where it was forced to be left off in January 2021.[354] In other words, when an administration is limited to one term in office, it truly has a compressed timeline to achieve things—particularly with elections always around the corner. But the Trump administration had developed a playbook to go into these communities, and Scott believes that mastering this playbook for future presidencies would yield tremendous benefits for these communities.[355] The workstreams associated with the WHORC's efforts focused on economic development and entrepreneurship, workforce and education, and public safety and community empowerment. And a number of key people were hired or otherwise brought into the White House from other agencies to ensure that connectivity was in place throughout the administration. As mentioned earlier, Charlotte, North Carolina, was the first location scheduled to be on the receiving end of these playbook efforts, and Miami, Florida, was soon to follow—but due to COVID, the efforts were cancelled.

This committed approach also led to the formal creation of the Opportunity Now initiative—the program Brooke Rollins had discussed with Chris after the meeting in Jared Kushner's office in December 2019. Opportunity Now sought to more efficiently and effectively align programs across all levels of government to maximize results to underserved communities. While there were a number of folks significantly engaged in the policy effort—including Brooke Rollins and Steve Smith—it was practically meant to be managed by Chris and Ja'Ron, with cross-country travels working with mayors and governors to advance federal, state, and local engagement across their communities. Of course, the pandemic

---

[354] Interview with Scott Turner, August 2022.
[355] Interview with Scott Turner, August 2022.

impacted the execution of this strategy, and while the engagement became mostly virtual, it led to partnerships that sought to achieve the same ends. Instead of convenings, Chris, Ja'Ron, Steve, and the team held conference calls with mayors, governors, nonprofits, think tanks, local economic officials, leaders of large corporations and churches, and many others to take in all of the information about how the federal government could specifically help these communities. Each elected leader indicated that their top three issues at any given time were health and safety, access to capital and jobs, and housing; and the White House team drilled down deeply into these topics and looked to see if any specific federal actions could be taken—related to federal grants, for example—or if the federal government could seek to partner cities that could mutually benefit from working with one another. For instance, one city might have a shovel-ready project but need access to workers and a training facility to advance it. The Opportunity Now team sought and acted upon that type of partnership to help these mayors govern at a time when small businesses were shuttering, tax revenues were dropping, and there were many more questions than answers available to them.

During that time, President Trump took steps to direct his administration and the WHORC to focus on support for underserved communities impacted so substantially during the pandemic. Some of the notable achievements of that period included:

- Providing at least 550,000 Black stakeholders with comprehensive, direct updates on preparedness, response, and mitigation efforts around the pandemic;
- Reaching hundreds of thousands of Hispanic stakeholders through conference calls, town halls, and virtual events to inform about our COVID-19 response;
- Holding weekly calls with tribal leaders to assist tribal communities with response, mitigation, and recovery efforts;

- Developing legislation to provide $60 billion in loans under the Paycheck Protection Program targeted to support minority and disadvantaged communities, as well as up to $1,200 in direct cash payments to Americans who had been affected by the COVID-19 pandemic and provided additional payments for their families;

- Temporarily delaying student loan repayments, holding interest rates at zero, and providing students with more than $6 billion in emergency assistance;

- Providing $1 billion to historically Black colleges and universities, Hispanic-serving institutions, and other minority-serving institutions that had experienced hardship due to COVID-19, and continued to target funds to institutions in need;

- Coordinating $3.5 billion to keep childcare centers open for low-income families and frontline workers;

- Halting evictions on federal government–assisted housing and temporarily preventing foreclosures for some Federal Housing Administration–insured mortgages;

- Committing to equipping underserved communities with the necessary testing and health care resources they needed to combat the COVID-19 pandemic;

- Investing approximately $2 billion in community health centers, helping their twenty-eight million patients in medically underserved areas receive the care and testing they needed;

- Developing legislation to guarantee coronavirus testing free of cost-sharing, removing financial obstacles for Americans who would otherwise be unable to access them;

- Devoting $2 billion to support hospitals with high COVID-19 admissions based on their Medicare and Medicaid disproportionate-share and uncompensated-care payments; and

- Removing financial hurdles to getting appropriate care, and federal government coverage of the cost of coronavirus treatment for uninsured patients. [356]

But the work did not stop there. It was also a time to look at big issues and seek partnerships with new and thoughtful leaders to help these communities. One of those partnerships was with the artist O'Shea Jackson Sr., more popularly known as Ice Cube. He and his longtime business manager and partner, Jeff Kwatinetz, connected with White House officials to advance opportunities for the Black community. Ice Cube and Jeff outlined their plan in a document titled a Contract with Black America (CWBA), laying out very specific policy goals that would advance these opportunities. For clarity, the goals were not political at all; they merely informed an approach they believed would help to level the economic and social playing fields. The CWBA included ways to reform credit and banking rules, criminal justice and housing laws, and many other areas, with the ultimate goal of passing legislation to support these initiatives.

As the CWBA was intended to be nonpartisan, Ice Cube's position was that whichever side of the aisle was engaged did not matter as long as the issues were addressed. Newspaper reports from 2020 indicate that then presidential candidate Joe Biden's team informed Ice Cube that they would connect with him after the election. Recognizing that the CWBA was about policy, and that the politics on these issues was irrelevant when one of two people was going to become president, Jeff Kwatinetz came into the White House for a meeting with Jared Kushner. Ja'Ron, Chris, and Steve Smith were asked to join that meeting. Sitting just outside the Navy Mess in the Ward Room, one of the smallest rooms in the West

---

[356] "President Donald J. Trump Is Committed to Providing Support to Underserved Communities Impacted by the Coronavirus Pandemic," May 13, 2020, https://trumpwhitehouse.archives.gov/briefings-statements/president-donald-j-trump-committed-providing-support-underserved-communities-impacted-coronavirus-pandemic/.

Wing, Kushner explained that the team was looking for a different way to help the Black community and was particularly interested in discussing the CWBA. To be clear, no one asked for an endorsement or any quid pro quo. Rather, the meeting was just for the White House to learn more about the CWBA plan and how to work with Ice Cube's team to advance its principles. That meeting lasted about ninety minutes.

After Kwatinetz left, the White House team considered what elements of the CWBA could potentially be advanced by the Trump administration, both by executive action and by legislation. There were a significant number of areas for potential engagement, and the team scheduled a follow-up call with Ice Cube and Kwatinetz. That call involved a bit more of feeling each other out. Just like with the First Step Act, a level of trust needed to be developed before folks went all in for this relationship. From there, documents and proposals were shared, and over the course of the next few calls, a real dialogue developed. Everyone was transparent as to the reality of what could be achieved. Ice Cube and Kwatinetz continued to push all of their ideas, but were very open to listening and considering alternatives as they became attuned to some of the potential bureaucratic hurdles. In one conversation, Ice Cube was mulling over some of the ideas being developed, and he explained that in order for him to support those ideas, he needed to be able to express the overall tenor of the plan with a "simple song." The concept made sense to everyone right away, as it was understood that he needed something that he could take to the Black community, a clear and direct headline of sorts from which everything else would develop, rather than the typical administrative political doublespeak. And that headline needed a real and significant all-in dollar figure. That was critical to Ice Cube and Kwatinetz. With a clear mandate, the work continued. And to be clear, the process was not about just writing a wish list; it involved a critical analysis of available funding and legislative realities. The work included hours and hours of meetings with the OMB and other key White House offices to ensure that the administration could make good on any proposal. Finally, just in time for an in-person meeting with Ice Cube and Kwatinetz, the administration had a viable plan to discuss.

When the administration's team initially approached Ice Cube about an in-person meeting, of course there was interest in having him come to the White House. But they all understood that he could face media backlash for it. Kushner therefore offered to meet at the Willard Hotel, located just east of the White House. On a hot afternoon in September 2020, Ice Cube and Kwatinetz welcomed the White House team to the Teddy Roosevelt Room on the ninth floor of the hotel, overlooking the World War I Memorial. The team included both Ja'Ron and Chris, as well as Kushner, Brooke Rollins, Steve Smith, and Nicole Frazier, a White House colleague who had been integral to this entire process.

The team brought poster boards and easels to present the idea, as well as all of the associated PowerPoint slides. Kushner led the presentation while Ice Cube and Kwatinetz studied the materials. As tends to occur in such a setting, the big ideas developed into conversations about the specific importance of these goals and the realistic ways they could be achieved. Ice Cube stressed that while he was supportive of opportunities for all underserved people, their efforts were focused on the Black community. The White House team certainly appreciated and respected that notion. And with his hair and beard grown out a bit, showing some gray, Ice Cube resembled something of a Frederick Douglass character, and seemed perhaps an unintentional civil rights leader for the modern era.

Once the news broke of the meeting, however, Ice Cube was publicly ridiculed by a small but vocal group of his fans, as well as some among the left-leaning media, for taking such a meeting, and his career may have been impacted at some level by his decision to work with the White House team. But Ice Cube is a man who has stood up for himself and his people many times before, and when someone on Twitter accused him of "working with the Darkside," he simply responded that "every side is the Darkside for us here in America. Our justice is bipartisan."[357]

Ultimately the "simple song" that would be delivered was a $500 billion plan for Black America, which would come to be known as the Platinum Plan. And it was not "pie in the sky" either. Every detail had been confirmed with the relevant leadership of all of the agencies and the OMB. In fact, Chris recalls being in his office with Steve Smith the evening they ran the final numbers to reach the half-trillion-dollar figure. The team had put so much effort into getting to that number that Chris and Steve decided to go get a beer to recognize the achievement.

As you may recall, the area outside the White House saw almost daily confrontations and potential violence during the summer of 2020. There were many protests and significant damage to buildings, as well as a steady stream of Secret Service personnel in full riot gear surrounding the modular gates that had been put up to protect the White House complex. The only bar that was open was the Blackfinn, a couple of blocks from the North Lawn of the White House. To get there, Chris and Steve walked past some of these Secret Service members, through the trophy corporate office space around the White House—much of which had had glass smashed, boarded up, and spray-painted by the public. As they walked to the bar, their excitement about having finally found the money to fund these efforts turned to somberness as they surveyed all of the damage and destruction surrounding them—much of it directed at a White House whose personnel had been privately working night and day to develop a half-trillion-dollar plan to begin to address some of the concerns of the protestors.

---

[357] "The Inside Story of How Ice Cube Joined Forces with Donald Trump," Politico, October 15, 2020, https://www.politico.com/news/2020/10/15/ice-cube-trump-partnership-429713.

The Platinum Plan was launched at an event in Atlanta in October 2020. It became the largest stand-alone proposal of all time to advance Black communities, which unfortunately seems to have gone unnoticed by much of the electorate. It had four key pillars—opportunity, security, prosperity, and fairness, and made several promises founded on that $500 billion commitment from the administration. The promises generally included: (1) three million new jobs; (2) the creation of five hundred thousand Black-owned businesses; (3) an increase of almost $500 billion in accessible capital; (4) safe neighborhoods with the highest policing standards; (5) the development of a Second Step Act on criminal justice reform; (6) access to better education and job training opportunities; (7) the ability for Black churches to compete for federal resources; (8) tailored health care to address historic disparities; (9) an immigration policy that would protect American jobs; (10) the advancement of home ownership and financial literacy; and (11) onshoring to advance opportunities for Black-owned businesses.[358]

A pretty comprehensive plan, yes? This framework was able to be envisioned, established, and implemented only by a cross-government plan and accountability by each agency and cabinet secretary. Each area of the plan underscored very specific action items, creating the kind of accountability that is often overlooked in political promises. For example, the jobs component was going to be supported by infrastructure funding as well as a dedicated corporate onshoring plan, and there was to be an OMB-approved $20 billion commitment to extending broadband to rural and underserved areas. Also included were access to capital mechanisms, to be buttressed by historic funding set aside for CDFIs and MDIs; codified credit-building alternatives; strategic mentor-protégé lending relationships; and quarterly accountability meetings with CEOs of major banks around their actions for underserved communities.

---

[358] "The Platinum Plan," Donald Trump for President, https://cdn.donaldjtrump.com/public-files/press_assets/president-trump-platinum-plan-final-version.pdf.

Other components of the plan included items that the Biden administration adopted, including making the Minority Business Development Agency permanent, making Juneteenth a national holiday, and making lynching a federal crime. Additional components included national prosecution of the KKK as a terrorist group, a clemency program to support the family structure, continuation of historic efforts for HBCUs, redoubled efforts on second-chance hiring, and historic investments for research into illnesses adversely impacting Black communities—including sickle cell disease, kidney disease, diabetes, and elements of maternal mortality. While this is just a snapshot, it shows some of the details that President Trump, his cabinet, and his staff committed to and were ready to execute, with responsible budgeting for each.

You can see in just those few sentences that this was the beginning of the Marshall Plan–style initiative that the Black community needed, and it set the stage to support other underserved communities with specific, achievable, and accountable plans. The Atlanta launch event for the Platinum Plan and the overall initiative received some press coverage, but anecdotal evidence demonstrates that much of the information did not get to the people who needed to hear it—the voters. This was not an election issue per se, but rather references how voters must be made aware of intentional policy commitments so that they can decide which candidates will advance—in this case—underserved communities. While the time for the Platinum Plan has passed, its legacy can live on in a way that embraces a commitment from civil society to advance opportunities for all.

CHAPTER **EIGHT**

The Role of Trauma in Underserved Communities

E veryone around the world felt the emotional and economic impacts
of the COVID pandemic. The emotional impact could have been as
basic as a loss of human contact or as extreme as exposure to violence or
self-harm. Those in underserved communities undoubtedly experienced
varying degrees of trauma more frequently and more significantly than
many other geographic areas, with the loss of jobs, businesses, residences,
and a certain level of control over everyday activities. There has of course
been significant academic research in the area of trauma, but our society's
anecdotal discussions around the concept tend to be more isolated on topics such as war or abuse. An area that is not often discussed is the role that
intergenerational trauma plays in our lives. This term refers to significant
emotional impact that transfers to one's children and beyond.[359] This type

---

[359] The American Psychological Association defines this as *"a phenomenon in
which the descendants of a person who has experienced a terrifying event show
adverse emotional and behavioral reactions to the event that are similar to those of
the person himself or herself."* Janice Gassam Asare, "3 Ways Intergenerational
Trauma Still Impacts the Black Community Today," *Forbes*, February 14, 2022,

of trauma can take many forms, but has often been recognized as passing generationally through the Black community as an impact of slavery.[360]

In her book, *Post Traumatic Slave Syndrome*, Joy DeGruy describes three critical components of this legacy on the modern Black community.[361] The first impact is on self-esteem, which she describes as a sort of "learned hopelessness"[362]—or "the perception that no matter what a person does, they cannot change their situation or condition. A person who feels learned helplessness, though frustrated, will stop trying to change their circumstances."[363] In the context of what has been discussed here so far, this is a very insightful concept. If a person truly believes this, then no government program will help that person think differently. Whereas the conservative icons discussed herein do not hesitate to account for the needs of the underserved in the greater policy framework, what do you do for those who simply are emotionally unable to grasp opportunity? It is a very difficult question to answer, but as we will discuss, developing a community of support—as opposed to dependence on government—may be impactful.

---

https://www.forbes.com/sites/janicegassam/2022/02/14/3-ways-intergenerational-trauma-still-impacts-the-black-community-today/?sh=4efa76583cf6.

[360] For Black Americans who descended from enslaved people, the trauma that was experienced by ancestors has been passed down through each generation. This trauma was explored in detail in the work of Dr. Joy DeGruy, who wrote the book *Post Traumatic Slave Syndrome: America's Legacy of Enduring Injury and Healing*. Asare, "3 Ways Intergenerational Trauma Still Impacts the Black Community Today."

[361] Asare, "3 Ways Intergenerational Trauma Still Impacts the Black Community Today."

[362] Asare, "3 Ways Intergenerational Trauma Still Impacts the Black Community Today."

[363] Asare, "3 Ways Intergenerational Trauma Still Impacts the Black Community Today."

The second component DeGruy discusses is the generational impact on the health of Black Americans.[364] Generational stressors have been shown to impact not just psychological and emotional states but also physical. In fact, they serve as a significant contributing factor to chronic ailments such as high blood pressure, hypertension, and accelerated biological aging.[365] She argues that this problem becomes exacerbated in underserved communities, where many people lack access to health care and where access to fresh and nutritious foods is not as common.[366] This point is also significant in that there are both genetic and lifestyle diseases that are more prevalent in the Black community—such as diabetes and stroke. By examining the root causes of these illnesses, one can more efficiently analyze access to the treatments and preventive care that can lead to a healthier community, which will then be better prepared to embrace social and economic opportunities.

The last component DeGruy discusses is the role of internalized oppression, which is simply the idea that someone does not deserve value or respect because of what they look like.[367] This can particularly be seen intergenerationally, as parents and grandparents share stories and experiences that last well beyond their years in the minds of their offspring. Simply hearing from trusted sources that this was their lot in life and will more than likely be yours too can of course be very limiting and depressing. And then, these same young people are impacted by interacting with their community of peers who are hearing the same thing from their older relatives and reacting with the same despair.

---

[364] Asare, "3 Ways Intergenerational Trauma Still Impacts the Black Community Today."

[365] Asare, "3 Ways Intergenerational Trauma Still Impacts the Black Community Today."

[366] Asare, "3 Ways Intergenerational Trauma Still Impacts the Black Community Today."

[367] Asare, "3 Ways Intergenerational Trauma Still Impacts the Black Community Today."

It is important to consider that in both rural and urban areas, parents of impoverished families can extend their stressors to their children in the form of severe discipline, low attention to developmental needs, outright neglect, and even physical violence.[368] Some of these circumstances begin with chaotic and disorganized lifestyles, which impact the family's ability to cope with crises and relationship conflicts.[369] And these circumstances often are exacerbated by previous trauma or life stressors that the supervising family members have experienced, including racial discrimination, social perceptions, depleted resources, and neighborhood criminal activity—all of which often perpetuate cycles of crisis. Research shows that approximately 49 percent of children in urban areas (numbering about ten million) are part of low-income families.[370] And as low-income families represent about 20 percent of the homeless in this country, these children often face heightened anxiety around where they will rest their heads on any given night.[371]

Moreover, these children face near-certain exposure to some sort of traumatic event, such as a shooting or stabbing.[372] And, as if all of this

---

[368] *"In the United States, almost 900,000 cases of neglect and abuse are substantiated yearly, with more than 300,000 youth placed in out-of-home care. Each year, 20– 35% of abused children suffer a serious injury and between 1,200 and 1,500 die as a result of abuse. One-third of individuals who were abused as children will become perpetrators of abuse in adulthood."* "Understanding the Impact of Trauma and Urban Poverty on Family Systems: Risks, Resilience and Interventions," Family Informed Trauma Treatment Center, 4, https://www.nctsn.org/sites/default/ files/resources/resource-guide/understanding_impact_trauma_urban_pov- erty_family_systems.pdf.

[369] "Understanding the Impact of Trauma and Urban Poverty on Family Systems: Risks, Resilience and Interventions."

[370] "Understanding the Impact of Trauma and Urban Poverty on Family Systems: Risks, Resilience and Interventions."

[371] "Understanding the Impact of Trauma and Urban Poverty on Family Systems: Risks, Resilience and Interventions."

[372] *"49% of American children in urban areas (9.7 million) live in low-income fam- ilies. Families of color are disproportionally represented in impoverished urban neighborhoods. Black and Latino families with children are more than twice as*

were not horrible enough, certain kinds of trauma within the family unit and some communities—such as gang violence and incarceration—can lead to a sort of post-traumatic stress disorder (PTSD).[373] This PTSD can in turn be exacerbated by the possible anticipatory anxiety that they deal with on a daily basis, which can account for innumerable fears and aggressive behaviors—all of which may seem to these children like normal responses to help them adapt to their environment.[374] Such deeply embedded experiences during a child's formative years often stunt childhood development socially and academically, as well as negatively

---

likely as white families with children to experience economic hardships. Families constitute two-fifths of the U.S. homeless population, which increases the risk of trauma exposure and intense anxiety and uncertainty. 83% of inner city youth report experiencing one or more traumatic events. 1 out of 10 children under the age of six living in a major American city report witnessing a shooting or stabbing. 59% - 91% of children and youth in the community mental health system report trauma exposure. 60% - 90% of youth in juvenile justice have experienced traumas. Urban males experience higher levels of exposure to trauma, especially violence related incidents." "Understanding the Impact of Trauma and Urban Poverty on Family Systems: Risks, Resilience and Interventions."

[373] *"These justice-involved youth witnessed and experienced high levels of violence likely to cause trauma. For example, almost one-half (49%) witnessed someone being shot, and 30% witnessed someone being killed. The symptoms most strongly associated with exposure to violence were hostility and paranoid ideation. The researchers found that adolescents who witnessed violence or were victimized by violence were more likely to be charged with a crime against a person at a later time. Court outcome severity was higher for this group—that is, youth exposed to violence in this sample experienced more adjudication, were more likely to be assigned to residential placement, and were more likely to be put on probation."* Phelan Wyrick and Kadee Atkinson, "Examining the Relationship Between Childhood Trauma and Involvement in the Justice System," National Institute of Justice, April 29, 2021, https://nij.ojp.gov/topics/articles/examining-relationship-between-childhood-trauma-and-involvement-justice-system.

[374] See generally "Understanding the Impact of Trauma and Urban Poverty on Family Systems: Risks, Resilience and Interventions."

affect their self-confidence and view of themselves.[375] And these children are not alone. Researchers estimate that up to 90 percent of all adults have endured a traumatic event, and up to 8 percent of those people will develop a condition that amounts to PTSD.[376] That said, impoverished adults in urban areas are more likely than other adults to develop trauma symptoms that impact their physical and mental health, influencing their ability to function in social and workplace environments.[377]

With the almost overwhelming specter of fears and anxieties presented by poverty, violence, and potential homelessness and abuse, an often-overlooked component of trauma and associated emotions is the distortive impact on economic decision-making. Research shows that job loss and decreased personal economic output lead to increased rates in depression.[378] For example, "areas in the USA more exposed to trade

---

[375] *"Finally, lowered future expectations are often formed as children with chronic trauma histories experience ongoing functional impairments, including substance abuse, delinquency, suicidality, acts of self-destruction, chronic anger, unstable relationships, and dissociation."* "Understanding the Impact of Trauma and Urban Poverty on Family Systems: Risks, Resilience and Interventions."

[376] Rubin Khoddam, "How Trauma Affects the Body," *Psychology Today*, March 3, 2021, https://www.psychologytoday.com/us/blog/the-addiction-connection/202103/how-trauma-affects-the-body#:~:text=An%20estimated%20 90%20percent%20of,develop%20PTSD%20during%20their%20lifetime.

[377] *"Furthermore, experiencing childhood abuse, neglect or other traumatic stressors, known as adverse childhood experiences, increases the individual's risk for a variety of health problems as an adult, including alcoholism, heart disease, obesity, drug use, liver disease, and depression, among others. Constant worry about hunger, violence, illness and accidents, economic strain, and discrimination experienced by those dealing with poverty-related stress has been tied to reduced physical and mental health such as depression and anxiety. Also, biological factors, such as allostatic load and predisposing genetic factors, may increase an individual's vulnerability to the development of PTSD."* "Understanding the Impact of Trauma and Urban Poverty on Family Systems: Risks, Resilience and Interventions," 22.

[378] Matthew Ridley, Gautam Rao, Frank Schilbach, and Vikram Patel, "Poverty, Depression, and Anxiety: Causal Evidence and Mechanisms," National Bureau

liberalization with China saw reduced income and employment for some groups of workers and increased mortality through drug overdoses among those same groups."[379] As we have discussed, impoverished families can experience anxiety and uncertainty daily, and this can cause other negative circumstances as well.[380] For instance, shame and isolation can result from low social status, due to comparisons with others in more stable circumstances.[381] These comparisons can create distorted images of one's situation and competencies.[382] And this distortion can become a vicious cycle, with negative experiences worsening the already present pessimism.

These individual circumstances affect the larger labor supply and, in turn, local, regional, and national productivity, given that individuals in this cycle might work less and less due to these feelings.[383] The associated social stigma can also lead them to seek positions, or force them to take positions, that pay lower wages and offer limited opportunities for advancement.[384]

Recognizing that the COVID pandemic's impacts on mental and behavioral health undoubtedly would become severe, on October 5, 2020, President Trump signed the executive order entitled Saving Lives Through

---

of Economic Research, November 2020, 22, https://www.nber.org/system/files/working_papers/w27157/revisions/w27157.rev0.pdf.

[379] Ridley, Rao, Schilbach, and Patel, "Poverty, Depression, and Anxiety: Causal Evidence and Mechanisms."

[380] See generally Ridley, Rao, Schilbach, and Patel, "Poverty, Depression, and Anxiety: Causal Evidence and Mechanisms."

[381] See generally Ridley, Rao, Schilbach, and Patel, "Poverty, Depression, and Anxiety: Causal Evidence and Mechanisms."

[382] Ridley, Rao, Schilbach, and Patel, "Poverty, Depression, and Anxiety: Causal Evidence and Mechanisms," 13.

[383] Ridley, Rao, Schilbach, and Patel, "Poverty, Depression, and Anxiety: Causal Evidence and Mechanisms," 13.

[384] Ridley, Rao, Schilbach, and Patel, "Poverty, Depression, and Anxiety: Causal Evidence and Mechanisms," 13.

Increased Support for Mental and Behavioral Health Needs.[385] While the concept had been considered internally at the White House Coronavirus Working Group, one catalyst for the effort came from Chris' conversation with Jared Kushner on that morning in June after Chris' brother's funeral, the events of which are discussed in more detail in the beginning of this book. At the time, the entire federal government was focusing its policies on physical and economic health. While various mental health/suicide prevention programs did exist within the federal agencies, this executive order helped to consolidate existing efforts and align future strategies to address the mental and behavioral health crisis, which was not only ongoing, but also deemed to be a potential crisis of unseen proportions once the early stages of COVID-related lockdowns were over.

The effort to advance this executive order was spearheaded by the DPC, led by Brooke Rollins at this time. Chris worked alongside White House colleagues Dr. Arthur Kleinschmidt and Marine reservist James Baehr. Kleinschmidt was a clinical therapist whose experience with at-risk communities was critical to a thoughtful advancement of this initiative, and Baehr had previously been instrumental in developing and implementing PREVENTS, a Department of Veterans Affairs–led suicide-prevention program.[386] Together, these three worked with all of the different agencies

---

[385] "Executive Order Saving Lives Through Increased Support for Mental and Behavioral Health Needs Report," December 2020, Substance Abuse and Mental Health Services Administration, https://www.samhsa.gov/sites/default/files/saving-lives-mental-behavioral-health-needs.pdf.

[386] *"The President's Roadmap to Empower Veterans and End a National Tragedy of Suicide (PREVENTS). Executive Order 13861, signed on March 5, 2019, created PREVENTS to implement an "all of nation" approach to prevent suicide and created an interagency task force to focus on this effort. It resulted in the development of a comprehensive plan, or Roadmap, to empower Veterans, and to end suicide for all Americans through culture change, seamless access to care, a connected research ecosystem, and robust community engagement."* "Executive Order Saving Lives Through Increased Support for Mental and Behavioral Health Needs Report," 6.

via an associated presidential coordinating committee, led by Dr. Elinore McCance-Katz, assistant secretary of the U.S. Department of Health and Human Services' Substance Abuse and Mental Health Services Administration (SAMSA). The executive order was then drafted, signed, and amplified through various reports, events, and other efforts across the administration—including efforts by Second Lady Karen Pence.

The executive order recognized that the COVID pandemic was forcing everything inside. People. Problems. Fears. And all of the associated impacts.[387] All most people could do was watch the news and hope that the pandemic would be over soon enough. In the midst of that, existing maladies endured, and fresh anxieties blossomed.[388] Stresses related to areas such as employment, finances, schooling, and the COVID illness itself stretched across every home in America. People of course communicated by phone or video chat, or existed within their so-called pods, but many people lost contact with friends, family, churches, temples, mosques, and their larger communities. The order sought to address some of those issues, coordinating all available resources for those who were

---

[387] *"Many people have been distanced from loved ones due to the risk of infection, and are fearful of contagion, death, and losing family and friends. As state and local governments mandated prolonged stay-at-home orders and forced non-essential businesses to close, the economy was put into decline, and millions of people also have been faced with the loss of their jobs, income, and homes."* "Executive Order Saving Lives Through Increased Support for Mental and Behavioral Health Needs Report," 4.

[388] *"Sixty-two percent of Americans have reported feeling more anxious this year compared with last year, according to a public opinion poll released recently by the American Psychiatric Association. 1 This is compared to data over the past three years, which demonstrates that between 32% and 39% of Americans report feeling more anxious compared with prior years. In fact, according to the Centers for Disease Control and Prevention (CDC) Morbidity and Mortality Weekly Report, at the end of June 2020, 40% of Americans reported experiencing significant emotional upheaval with anxiety, depression, trauma-related symptoms, increased use of substances and even suicidal ideation (11% reported seriously considering suicide), which was a higher percentage than in the previous year."* "Executive Order Saving Lives Through Increased Support for Mental and Behavioral Health Needs Report," 3.

facing them—and specifically for those who were turning to alcohol, drugs, or self-harm as a way to cope.

While the order estimated that the impacts of the COVID pandemic could lead to much-needed treatment for millions of Americans, it focused on many of the truly vulnerable populations—such as minorities, seniors, veterans, small business owners, children, those impacted by domestic abuse, those addicted to drugs and alcohol, and those with disabilities. It also included support for frontline workers, who were working countless hours through the height of the COVID pandemic—very often under the stresses of exhaustion and fears of illness and death.[389] And much like he did with the WHORC, the cabinet-level council discussed earlier, President Trump established a government-wide Coronavirus Mental Health Working Group, which would be responsible for identifying all agency programs and resources, prioritizing ongoing efforts on pandemic-related issues, and working with both public and private stakeholders to address these imminent needs. Once again, this demonstrates the philosophy of the all-in approach—one that includes government but stresses that the engagement of the private sector, religious organizations, and nonprofit communities is critical.

Much like the intergenerational trauma that undoubtedly now exists from the COVID pandemic, the additional factor of poverty has impacted and will continue to impact so many peoples' lives and interactions with others, as well as their own families' economic decision-making, as they make their way in a post-pandemic world. Experts fear that the economic and social impacts of the pandemic will either exacerbate or uncover previously unknown instances of child abuse, addiction, and family instability, some of which may have been present at some level even before the pandemic. These types of traumas will undoubtedly affect growing children and young adults, and may even lead to more of the intergenerational

---

[389] See generally "Executive Order Saving Lives Through Increased Support for Mental and Behavioral Health Needs Report."

concerns that have already been discussed. Of course, poverty can also play a significant exacerbating role here, and plans that support economic opportunity may serve as an important factor to ultimately promote access to resources and some healing among those affected. [390]

With this recognition that there is an existing mental health crisis in this country, and one that could become even more significant given the impacts of the pandemic, any plan for underserved communities must be thoughtful about the mental health component of economic mobility and ensure that a meaningful approach prioritizes those we are trying to support. Whether it includes histories of violence,[391] drug problems, [392]

---

[390] Research published in National Library of Science states that an estimated *"37.4% of all children experience a child protective services investigation by age 18 years. Consistent with previous literature, they found a higher rate for African American children (53.0%) and the lowest rate for Asians/Pacific Islanders (10.2%)."* Hyunil Kim, Christopher Wildeman, Melissa Jonson-Reid, and Brett Drake, "Lifetime Prevalence of Investigating Child Maltreatment Among U.S. Children," *American Journal of Public Health* (February 2017), https://www.ncbi.nlm.nih.gov/pmc/articles/PMC5227926/.

[391] *"Crime rates changed dramatically across the United States in 2020. Most significantly, the murder rate — that is, the number of murders per 100,000 people — rose sharply, by nearly 30 percent. Assaults increased as well, with the rate of offenses rising by more than 10 percent."* Ames Grawert, "Myths and Realities: Understanding Recent Trends in Violent Crime," Brennan Center for Justice, https://www.brennancenter.org/our-work/research-reports/myths-and-realities-understanding-recent-trends-violent-crime.

[392] Center for Disease Control also reported that in *"the first full year of the pandemic in the United States, through April 2021, more than 99,000 people died from drug overdoses. This represents an increase of nearly 30% from the 77,000 who died in the previous 12 months. The CDC also reported that approximately 75% of overdose deaths during the pandemic's first year were tied to synthetic opioids, such as fentanyl. There has also been an increase in the abuse of many other drugs since the pandemic began in 2020, including heroine, methamphetamines, and cocaine."* "Substance Use Has Risen During COVID-19 Pandemic," Republican Policy Conference, March 15, 2022, https://www.rpc.senate.gov/policy-papers/substance-use-has-risen-during-covid-19-pandemic.

attempted suicide,[393] or other issues, we must account not only for those individuals, but for the cycle of trauma, which can spread to those close to them. There is an old adage that "hurt people hurt people," and a holistic solution that accounts for trauma and mental health has to be at the foundation for any strategy to support underserved communities.

To create this foundation, the authors once again point to a model of civil society that leans on components such as the faith community as proven sources of support for healing from compounded trauma. Ja'Ron can speak to this firsthand, given the impact that the church had on his life during his own struggles with alcohol and the criminal justice system. He often looks back on particular verses of the Bible to remind him of that healing and how he is now in a position to pay it forward to those around him.[394] Redemption is a very personal experience, but being surrounded by those who wish to help you redeem and achieve is essential to the human experience, to the American experience. This is why community and civil society are both so important—getting back to a time when people checked in on their neighbors and looked after one another. This idea is the basis for the strategy of how conservatives can meet this moment head-on. Just as with the First and Second Great Awakenings in early American history, which ushered in the abolitionist movement and the end of slavery, religious institutions can help transform the heart of underserved communities today.

---

[393] It is estimated that twelve million individuals per year contemplate taking their own life; there are over one million failed attempts. "Facts About Suicide," Centers for Disease Control and Prevention, https://www.cdc.gov/suicide/facts/index.html#:~:text=Suicide%20rates%20increased%2030%25%20between,one%20death%20every%2011%20minutes.&text=The%20number%20of%20people%20who,attempt%20suicide%20is%20even%20higher.

[394] In the Bible, Mark 1:15 states, *"The time is fulfilled, and the kingdom of God is at hand; repent and believe in the gospel,"* and Romans 12:2 reads, *"Do not be conformed to this world, but be transformed by the renewal of your mind, that by testing you may discern what is the will of God, what is good and acceptable and perfect."*

CHAPTER **NINE**

A Plan to Complete the Vision of Lincoln's Reconstruction for Modern America

Conservative thinker Edmund Burke once said, "Nobody made a greater mistake than he who did nothing because he could do only a little."[395] The authors contend that the totality of the approach outlined herein will have a comprehensive impact for underserved communities. But the plan is not just for the federal government; it is also for the American people to hold their leaders accountable. And why is that? To quote Milton Friedman once again, "Governments never learn. Only people learn."[396] If those elected are not held accountable that the commitments they make to us are based on a specific plan, then we as an electorate have only ourselves to blame when officials show no real progress on those commitments. It is often assumed that just because someone has the moxie to put their name on the ballot and somehow get

---

[395] "Edmund Burke Quotes," https://www.azquotes.com/quote/41740.

[396] Ben Duronio, "9 Unforgettable Quotes from Milton Friedman," Business Insider, July 31, 2012, https://www.businessinsider.com/milton-friedman-quotes-2012-7.

the support of a local or national party, they deserve our vote. But society must look deeper and demand not only the results but the commitment to intentionality that drives success. This book has admittedly focused on Black people, but the all-in effort must be applied to all underserved communities—including all minorities, indigenous peoples, rural communities, and the economically disadvantaged—and go beyond race and socioeconomic status to assist the disabled and other at-risk populations.

As this book has demonstrated, underserved communities face innumerable economic and business challenges. For example, recent McKinsey studies show that 65 percent of Black Americans live in the sixteen states with below-average optimal circumstances for economic opportunity.[397] Further, these studies demonstrate the existence of entrepreneurial headwinds of historic discrimination that limit people's willingness to even engage in traditional business ecosystems,[398] as well as limited access to technical assistance specific to their venture.[399] These issues are compounded by systemic hiring challenges and a lack of mutually beneficial business relationships, as well as additional hurdles that

---

[397] David Baboolall, Kelemwork Cook, Nick Noel, Shelley Stewart, and Nina Yancy, "Building Supportive Ecosystems for Black-Owned US Businesses," McKinsey & Company, October 29, 2020, https://www.mckinsey.com/industries/public-and-social-sector/our-insights/building-supportive-ecosystems-for-black-owned-us-businesses.

[398] Baboolall, Cook, Noel, Stewart, and Yancy, "Building Supportive Ecosystems for Black-Owned US Businesses."

[399] *"Black entrepreneurs tend to make decisions in the business-ideation stage that are likely to keep their businesses small.... Black entrepreneurs can also have difficulty accessing expertise and business services. Black owners of employer firms, which are more likely to benefit from services such as legal and financial advisory, are less likely to seek them out. Only 58 percent of Black owners sought professional services, for reasons including expense, inaccessibility, and mistrust, compared with 70 percent of white owners."* "Building Supportive Ecosystems for Black-Owned US Businesses."

make it difficult to scale a business.[400] All of these limitations have been significant factors in creating the current wealth gap for Black communities and in other underserved populations.[401] For the reasons set

---

[400] *"Black entrepreneurs might also lack access to the networks and relationships that could help them make optimal business decisions. Research on New York–based start-ups shows that founders who are mentored by top-performing entrepreneurs are three times more likely than their co-located peers without mentors to become top performers themselves. Outside the start-up world, a knowledgeable contact may help a prospective entrepreneur make decisions such as whether to buy a franchise for up-front capital or to build an independent business. … Friends and family may not be able to contribute capital either. Most Black families surveyed said that they didn't know anyone who could lend them $3,000."* "Building Supportive Ecosystems for Black-Owned US Businesses."

[401] *"Lower levels of earnings for Black households account for about two-thirds of the average wealth gap, while the remainder is largely explained by financial factors, including access to capital and investment opportunities, personal finances, financial information, and housing. Black women make less in the labor market, primarily because they are paid significantly less per hour and also because they are 10 percentage points less likely to be employed than white men. The hourly earnings gap or "wage gap" of Black women stands at 15% relative to white women and 35% relative to white men. The wage gap of Black women widens through their whole work-life and especially rapidly between ages 20 and 35. Earnings gap is widening again. Using a statistical model, we find that improved access to better-paying occupations and industries drove a substantial narrowing in the wage gap of Black women relative to white men in the 80s and 90s. Unfortunately, progress in closing the wage gap of Black women vs. white men has stalled over the last two decades. The wage gap of Black women relative to white women stood at 5% in the early 80s when it was largely explained by differences in education, occupations, and industries. While these factors remain critical today, the wage gap has now grown to 15% on account of other harder-to-measure factors, which could capture differences in career opportunities, school quality, or bias and discrimination. This underscores the need to listen to Black women to fully understand their disadvantages and, critically, to address bias and discrimination. Capital access gap fuels wealth gap. Largely because of lower earnings and limited access to capital, Black Americans are much less likely to own high-return assets than white individuals, including homes, stocks, and especially their own businesses. The fact that Black women entrepreneurs cite limited access to funds as the largest barrier to success and that Black*

forth herein, rural communities have struggled as well, and while any strategic plan must incorporate ideas such as availability of technical job skill training in high schools, community college engagement, state workforce development board alignment, and reciprocity/recognition of occupational licensing across all states, certain other foundational factors must be addressed as well.

According to a report from the Stanford University Center on Poverty and Inequality, "when compared to 24 middle-income and high-income countries, the U.S. ranks 16th in the category of intergenerational earnings mobility."[402] Since the summer 2020 protests, the idea of how to create a social impact that would allow for more equity in underserved communities has become a focal point of many corporate responsibility and sustainability efforts by Fortune 500 companies. Conservatives have debated the notions of wokeness and woke corporations, but without a doubt, the private sector must play a critical role in reestablishing the concept of the civil society that the authors have conveyed in this book in order to achieve robust prosperity in underserved communities. The system of capitalism that has allowed these companies to achieve so much

---

entrepreneurs are 20% less likely to fund their startups with bank business loans suggest that capital access gaps contribute to the business ownership gap. Moreover, single Black women are four times less likely to inherit assets than single white men, which further perpetuates the wealth gap across generations. Personal finances gap. Black women's wealth is not only held down by a lower access to high-return assets, but also by a higher exposure to high-cost liabilities. Black women are, for instance, five times more likely than white men to rely on expensive payday loans, likely due to limited access to formal credit and potentially financial information gaps. Survey evidence on compound interest and familiarity with stock market risk suggest that Black women face a financial information gap." See Gizelle George-Joseph and Daniel Milo, *"Black Womenomics: Equalizing Entrepreneurship,"* February 9, 2022, Goldman Sachs, https://www.goldmansachs.com/insights/pages/gs-research/black-womenomics-equalizing-entrepreneurship/report.pdf.

[402] "Social Mobility," Stanford Center on Poverty & Inequality, https://inequality.stanford.edu/taxonomy/term/35.

can also provide for greater social impact than any other economic system in human history, because it gives citizens the greatest opportunity to pursue their dreams.

To ensure that the benefits of capitalism are accessible to underserved communities, any plan that incorporates the private sector must begin by focusing on the practical application of the social component of ESG, so that corporations as well as the broader community and its stakeholders reap the benefits. The goal is to create mutual value for all parties involved. Based on their time in the White House, in the Small Business Administration, on Capitol Hill, and in the private sector, the authors have designed a strategy for closing the economic mobility gap by implementing a road map to modernize the government's policies for underserved communities. The goal here is to develop a place-based approach to revitalizing low- to moderate-income communities through developing private sector coalitions that will pilot a new holistic infrastructure for opportunity. The practical model for this includes the following five components.

1. **Intentionality.** This refers to being deliberate and purposeful in working toward a particular goal. That process must include a clear focus on the problem to solve, a list of the particular marketplace advantages, a description of what capabilities can be leveraged to advance the public good, and finally, an acceptance of whatever is required to achieve the goal. To be intentional is to begin with the end in mind and to be laser-focused on whatever it takes to solve an issue. In America, the government and corporations know where the poor communities are and where economic development is needed, but what is being done to solve the issue of inequality? Each corporate partner that wants to offer solutions to these issues must first determine their comparative advantage in the marketplace and how they can offer a

unique value proposition in a way that creates more value for the company while providing value for the underserved community at the same time. The concept of capitalism is what makes this system work, because its perfect result is mutual benefit.

2. **Trust**. As in any relationship, this is developed through listening, learning, and communicating clearly and honestly. Among the parties, whether they be community leaders or those within the community itself, the ability to openly exchange both negative and positive information and count on the other party is very powerful in advancing goals. Steps to take in this effort include seeking to build credibility and authenticity, examining the entirety of the relationship and seeking to account for any blind spots or areas that may lead to confrontation, creating clarity around who will be impacted by the actions, and sharing information about the resources and assets that will be brought to bear to achieve the goal. At the end of the day, trust involves mutual respect and the confidence that each party will do what it says it will do. Building trust in the community is important to ensure that capitalism is viewed not as exploitative but as a foundation on which to build. Trust within a particular community must be built both internally and externally. Generations of politicians and businesspeople have exploited underserved communities for their own gain. So many communities do not trust external parties, fearing that they have no genuine concern for them. These communities want to see beneficial investments and positive outcomes for themselves and their neighbors. They want to know that if partners make an investment, they are doing so because they authentically believe the result will be mutually beneficial. So credibility needs to be built into any such transaction, and this must start with engaged and transparent listening sessions among all of the stakeholders, to develop a shared strategy with a mutually desirable outcome.

3. **Collaboration**. This refers to strategic partnerships among the stakeholders and a common commitment to maximize their capabilities for the greater good. With these issues, a whole host of potential collaborators exist, including the federal government, state and local government entities, private sector entities, the nonprofit community, religious organizations, colleges and universities, and community leaders. With well-positioned collaborators who maintain comparative advantages as partners, communities can make sure that their own outcomes are aligned with their partners' goals. Most often, a place-based approach supported by state and national partners is ideal because the solutions should be built up from the local community. The local, state, and federal governments need to be aligned so the private sector will know how to scale in the most efficient way possible—accounting for regulatory clarity and agreement among the governing bodies. Collaborations have to be mutually beneficial and market-oriented to be self-sustainable—another key reason to have the private sector take the lead in this return to a civil society that concentrates on innovation around access and opportunity, as opposed to an overwhelming morass of typical bureaucratic government programs. The government is of course a partner, but churches, nonprofits, and companies, including small businesses, should lead, because they are closer to those most significantly impacted. These entities have staying power because they are unelected and their own sustainability and continuity are dependent on outcomes in the marketplace.

4. **Outcomes**. In advocacy work, identified outcomes can include the results of the communication among parties; the enactment of a high-level policy approach, legislative items, or regulatory actions; an investment or a donation; infrastructure development; or simply a convening to initiate a dialogue. These types of outcomes are key to sustaining support for any plan that seeks to

provide stated and timely deliverables and milestones. Outcomes must be documented, adhered to, and set as the standard of success in order for this strategy to work. Historically, various government programs have allocated resources toward different strategies to fix the plight of underserved communities, but the resources have not been tied to outcomes, so the problems never get fixed. As a result, the funding has created a dependent web of unaccountable organizations that survive off these federal dollars without having to answer for what they fail to achieve. This only extends the cycle of dependence that has been discussed within this book. In short, while the outcomes may vary, the path to any particular goal must be clear and the intended outcome must be known to all, so that, if necessary, the strategy can be more efficiently amended to achieve the desired success.

5. **Data collection**. It is sometimes said that until someone can show something, it does not exist. And that really is true when it comes to policy. Developing specific data and an actionable plan for collecting it is critical for success in supporting an approach that will have a foreseeable impact on the matter at hand. Data provides the transparency that allows stakeholders to trust the plan that is being proposed, as it must be tied to the specific problem. It is different from outcomes in that in its raw form, data can inform a number of outcomes. Further, to avoid the criticism that data can be manipulated to tell stories that advance differing narratives—in other words, for any data-informed approach to be bipartisan and evergreen—not only must data be collected and measured appropriately, but the collection methodologies themselves must be discussed and agreed to by all involved parties in advance.

By incorporating intentionality, trust, collaboration, outcomes, and data collection as a practical framework, one can begin to build a strategy that will create better results for underserved communities. To demonstrate how this works, let us look again at the topic of HBCU funding. With the intention of ensuring that these schools would not have to apply yearly for funding, the Trump administration developed a level of trust with a number of stakeholders, such as the Thurgood Marshall College Fund and several of the HBCUs themselves. Data collection on the impact of these schools was significant, and but for President Trump's actions, a number of schools would have been in jeopardy due to loans that they could not repay or operational budgets they simply could not fund. With the Trump administration providing multiyear funding, HBCU leaders could focus their efforts on their schools' internal activities, as well as plan for future operational requirements.

This process was just as apparent with the First Step Act. Criminal justice reform legislation had not been passed in almost thirty years, and as discussed, the prior 1994 legislation led to significant growth of the prison population and did little to minimize recidivism among the incarcerated. The clear intention was to pass reform legislation that would create a more holistic and sustainable situation. While multiple groups were at the table, many of them were suspicious of one another. That said, they were willing to engage in a process to listen and learn, and eventually grew to trust one another—a point that was clear when they were able to openly discuss possibilities without fear of leaking and a media backlash that would have undercut the effort. Seeking a specific goal brought together Republicans, Democrats, conservatives, progressives, community groups, and law enforcement—all of whom agreed that the data supported the need for this reform. And the evidence demonstrates that this support for reform continues with President Biden's executive order on policing, which speaks to the ongoing importance of advancing the First Step Act as a critical part of the nation's criminal justice framework.

Now that an appropriate analytical policy framework has been described, let us turn our attention to the social ills that make up much of the foundational issues set forth in this book. Whether they address a lack of access to capital or employment, or generations of economic and social trauma, the lanes to achieve these goals must be created. For our analytical purposes, those lanes are as follows: safe and healthy communities; education and workforce development; economic development and affordability; and entrepreneurship and wealth-building. These four areas highlight the key overarching issues impacting underserved communities, as well as provide for the central policy topics that can be supported by an ecosystem of committed stakeholders seeking market-driven mutual benefit, namely federal, state, and local governments; the private sector (churches, companies, small businesses, and nonprofits); and the underserved.

Let's look at each of these four lanes individually.

1. **Safe and healthy communities**. Public health and public safety form the cornerstone of revitalization. Although public health has many elements, the focus within this plan would be mental health. The coalition addressing this would build off the work around police reform, violence reduction, and recidivism reduction. To achieve safe and healthy communities, there must be a focus on strengthening relationships between law enforcement and the local communities. The coalition would be composed of intentionally recruited local leaders and organizations who have the trust of the community, and their partners. The call to action can first focus on coordinating mental health professionals and/or faith institutions to help those within the community affected by generational trauma, mental illness, and addiction, with the main goal focusing on self-actualization.

   The Trump administration moved in this direction through the executive order Saving Lives Through Increased Support for Mental and Behavioral Health Needs, in October 2020, and by working with experienced and trusted national and local non-profit groups, a coalition can be built to strengthen and fortify underserved communities like never before. Ideally, multiple entities will be interested in convening to discuss public safety solutions. This coalition would create grassroot solutions in cities where reform is essential, and once it rolls out its proposed solutions with supporting data, that data will be used to help Congress create policies around police reform, mental health, and employment. In the current Congress, senators on both sides of the aisle have been champions on these issues, and are looking for ideas such as the ones discussed in this book to help solidify sound policy backed by real-world data. Once again, the private sector can be the leader on this by instituting the pilot programs and providing Congress with that data so that informed policy can be acted upon in the near term.

2. **Education and workforce development.** Although many businesses appear to be reopening post-pandemic, they are facing unprecedented challenges trying to find enough workers to fill open jobs. By partnering with companies in the technology, financial services, manufacturing, and energy sectors, to name just a few, workforce development advocates and the associated nonprofit ecosystem will be well positioned to address these shortages. Much like the approaches of the programs related to the Pledge to America's Workers, a systematic approach that educates and credentials workers to the specifications of a particular employment opportunity is the exemplar of mutual benefit. Many employers argue that too many candidates within the workforce pipeline have drug issues, problems showing up to work on time, or issues dealing with office conflict. Building off work to be done in the public safety component of this effort, helping more people join the workforce will help to offset criminal behavior, which in turn will impact some of the behaviors that stem from

social traumas that can lead to poor economic decision-making. It is critical to place emphasis on the mental health and past traumas of the targeted workforce, as these issues can play a large role in work productivity. Private companies have a vested interest in continuing to invest in this ecosystem, as their return on this investment would be a sustained, competent workforce. Along with the corporate partners, engagement here can come from minority-serving institutions, churches, and a whole host of organizations whose missions align with this effort.

3. **Economic development and affordability.** The focal point of this component is municipalities, cities, commercial developers, housing advocates, energy companies, and social services. Along with better access to education and workforce opportunities, people need affordable housing, quality schools, childcare, an environmentally friendly infrastructure (clean water and clean air), and access to transportation. To achieve these goals, society needs the private sector and the public sector to work hand in glove. Private capital is extremely important because public money is rarely there to modernize underserved areas. However, expansion of opportunity zones will help scale public-private partnerships to solve the economic development and affordability issues facing underserved communities. By beginning with pilot programs that incorporate trust and collaboration, both urban and rural cities will benefit when private sector engagement is present and incentivized, allowing for optimal business opportunities for, and not at the expense of, the residents of a particular area.

4. **Entrepreneurship and wealth-building.** This initiative will be focused on financial literacy, access to capital, and business profitability mentorships on a grassroots level. By establishing a coalition that includes financial services firms, the intention is to benefit local communities by teaching them how to access capital as well as build financial freedom through a proper understanding

of the financial system. This builds off the other three lanes and allows for generational wealth-building—whether it involves building a business, selling a business, making smart investments, owning a home, or a whole host of other possibilities. Building wealth, unlike intergenerational trauma, permits an aspirational legacy among families that can change the entire dynamic for underserved communities.

While the components of intentionality, trust, collaboration, outcomes, and data collection serve as constants in any policy equation, the four other areas listed above are specific to the topic of underserved communities. The table below shows how one might think about approaching the four goals based on the five components.

Examples of Potential Plans

	Safe and Healthy Communities	Education and Workforce Development	Economic Development and Affordability	Entrepreneurship and Wealth-Building
Intentionality	Stop violent crime	Create job opportunities in five low-income areas	Redevelop five neighborhoods without necessarily gentrifying the community	Establish a usable ecosystem of entrepreneurial training, access to capital, and financial literacy education
Trust	Listen to community leaders, police, and mental health professionals	Conduct a listening tour of employers, churches, elected officials and other stakeholders	Host community forums with elected officials, community leaders, business owners, and developers to learn where investments could advance the community	Leverage leaders who maintain trust in the community (e.g., pastors and local businesspeople) to serve as liaisons for this program

	Safe and Healthy Communities	Education and Workforce Development	Economic Development and Affordability	Entrepreneurship and Wealth-Building
Collaboration	Partner with groups to develop evidence-based solutions	Work with these groups to develop a pipeline to match people and job op-portunities through workforce training	Bring investors, the community, and other stake-holders together to establish a mutually beneficial revitalization plan	Establish engage-ment between local leaders and national nonprofits who have a record of providing capital access and financial education services
Outcomes	Enact a law; launch a pilot program	Produce five distinct cohorts of new em-ployees from low-income areas	Create more op-portunities for local residents, and local regulations supporting people's efforts to remain in the community	Pass laws that create incentives for finan-cial education
Data Collection	Certify if the law or pilot program ac-tually works and violent crime has been reduced	Assess the ability of employees to maintain jobs and/or be promoted	Analyze the com-ponents of the growing economy, e.g., new busi-nesses created and jobs established	Track wealth growth of cohorts that have utilized these services

So how can this plan be taken to market to bring all of the stakehold-ers together in a systematic and committed way? Starting with intention-ality, one must define the specific goal to be achieved. The complicated and simple answer is to establish and implement a market-based solution to advance the plight of underserved communities. In the context of pol-icy, what does this mean? It means that everyone—whether Democrat, Republican, or something else—has to acknowledge that this issue must be addressed. While people may have their own reasons for addressing the issue, such as its economic significance or simply just the right thing to do, they all must agree that it must be done, and must be willing to trust one another in a good-faith collaboration to find a way to do it. And while the particular position they take may be good politics, they must consciously commit to policies to address this problem; a bipartisan handshake will not suffice here. Rather, from a government perspective, all involved must demonstrate on the record commitment, coupled with a limited administrative budget and accompanying legislation to achieve that end.

Congress would begin by creating a bipartisan committee on underserved communities, which would be announced by leadership as the most bipartisan and engaged effort since World War II—noting that just as with the Marshall Plan, the effort must succeed to advance world order, as it is the promise of America that its democracy can evolve and its people can come together when its own future is at stake. Once this committee has been established, its members would lay out very clearly what issues they are trying to solve as opposed to making general statements about economic well-being. They would walk through all of the steps listed above to craft legislation that would reflect the needs, solutions, and associated metrics required to meet their goals. Part of this legislation would include a provision for a new federal government position—such as a tsar for underserved communities (TUC).

The TUC would be appointed by the president and require Senate approval with a two-thirds supermajority. That person would be in that position for a term of seven to ten years, much like the tenure given to the director of the Federal Bureau of Investigation, in order to account for continuity and limited political disruption. Once the TUC is in place, the White House would work with Congress to place all programs and agencies that impact the underserved under this individual. Housing all of these programs in one place would minimize redundancies, allow deregulatory opportunities to be identified, limit bureaucratic challenges, and streamline budgets and resources, as well as remove the common problem of one agency just simply not knowing that a complementary program exists at a sister agency. The TUC would establish advisory committees composed of members of underserved communities as well as academic, corporate, and other relevant stakeholders—all of whom would meet in a transparent fashion. Not unlike the teams involved in the Community Reinvestment Act and the creation of opportunity zones, these committees would assist in the development of outcome-based programming that would account for an incentive structure for private sector engagement, limited regulatory hurdles, and enhanced public-private engagement initiatives.

While some may criticize the creation of yet another government position as just more bureaucracy, the TUC role is critical to the success of this plan, as the program needs a leader who can avoid politics but still serve at a level that commands the respect and engagement of cabinet members and members of Congress in any administration. It does not mean that this role would exist forever; in fact, the legislation should indicate that it would sunset at a certain point if certain measurable outcomes are not achieved. Why should there be a provision for the role's elimination? Because the purpose of this approach is not to create another government program that goes on in perpetuity and supports the same cycle of dependence that other government programs have supported for decades. As the program must be outcome-based, its leaders would be held to quantitative achievements and standards that could inform the most casual observer as to how well the approach is working.

But if there is concern about adding to the perpetual government programs, why propose this program at all? The answer is simple, and it is the most basic point of this book. Reconstruction had the ability to set Black people and poor Southern Whites on a trajectory that would have allowed them to be competitive and engaged in civil society. The failures of that time have exacerbated poverty, economic trauma, familial instability, and so many other critical elements that the impact has risen to a true market failure for civil society. By taking a different approach today, we would collectively and intentionally take a massive step—albeit focused in scope and limited in duration—to turn the page on decades of disappointment, fear, and despair. And the good news is that we can start right now. As suggested by Milton Friedman, "Only a crisis—actual or perceived—produces real change. When that crisis occurs, the actions that are taken depend on the ideas that are lying around. That, I believe, is our basic function: to develop alternatives to existing policies, to keep them alive and available until the politically impossible becomes the politically inevitable."[403]

---

[403] "Milton Friedman in His Own Words," University of Chicago, https://mfidev. uchicago.edu/about/tribute/mfquotes.shtml.

AFTERWORD

Lessons that Must Be Heeded for This Plan to Succeed

As the authors, Chris and Ja'Ron, write this from the Eastern Shore of Maryland and just outside the District of Columbia, respectively, it is notable that the former location is the birthplace of Frederick Douglass and the latter is the birthplace of so much of the legislation and so many of the policies that have been explored in this book. It is clear that the failure of Reconstruction can be attributed to the imbalance of key ingredients—too much politics and too little committed intentionality, collaboration, and trust. Due to Lincoln's death, clear outcomes for Reconstruction were all but shelved by President Johnson, and without that vision, none of those ingredients could be effectively implemented. While so many from that time to the present have fought for various freedoms and opportunities, we now stand in the unique position to clearly articulate a comprehensive and intentional plan with specific results for underserved communities.

Any experienced policy person will know that this plan is not without its flaws, but that same person must also agree that the status quo simply cannot continue. If it does, underserved communities are going to remain the perennial victims of the cycle of dependency, and the taxpayers are going to continue to fund programs that go nowhere. It may not seem like a crisis—not like a war, a pandemic, a natural disaster, or a stock market failure—but it is a crisis that if left unaddressed will continue to undermine our civil society and so much of what we stand for as a country. We are of course not in a civil war, but we are in a time when the country is so strongly divided that actions must speak louder than words—because today's words are often not thoughtful and action-oriented, but rather barbs and placation aimed at an existing political base, and most important, often have no immediate consequence other than to benefit the speaker. Even in his own times, Lincoln recognized this kind of posturing. He of course had to handle the politics of war, but just two days after the war was over, he publicly endorsed the concept of the Black vote. And just three days after that, he was killed for those same remarks by a man who had been in the audience when he publicly took that stand. It may seem trite to refer to Lincoln as a hero—America already knows he was a hero. But it begs the question of who will be heroic now and pick up the mantle of the progress he intended to set into motion.

The Civil War era had numerous iconic figures, Lincoln chief among them. And the policy issues discussed here have had the support of massive figures of their day—presidents such as Franklin Roosevelt, Lyndon Johnson, Ronald Reagan—and as evidenced by just some of the information contained herein, much of the work of the Trump administration sought to embrace that legacy. Within this book, the reader has been presented with statements from famed conservative theorists who uniformly recognize that there is an important place in the conservative platform for underserved communities. But ultimately, this undertaking must be advanced by a mandate of the American people to an engaged

Congress and a visionary president, and under the direction of a committed manager of this sacred responsibility.

In the 1860s, a manager in a similar role was Major General Oliver Howard, the head of the Freedmen's Bureau. A West Point graduate and famed Army general, he was appointed by President Andrew Johnson to see to the welfare of millions of humans. While his tenure has been criticized for mismanagement, he fed millions of indigent people, provided medical aid, built hospitals, supported labor contracts for the freedmen, established many schools, and helped found one of the most well-known HBCUs, Howard University.[404] Just imagine the overwhelming responsibility of this role. As a military person, he certainly saw it as a duty, and perhaps as a religious man, he saw it the same way. He viewed this effort as being collaborative and truly American, stating, "The only way to lift the ponderous load of poverty from the houses of the poor whites and blacks, and keep it lifted is by instruction. I do not mean simply what is learned from books, but what is gained by example."[405]

While Howard likely knew that his role and agency would be limited, his orders were clear: to transition the Black community into a scenario where they could thrive as a people. No one knew what the blueprint should be; however, he was willing to pick up the mantle to do it. You don't hear much about him in the history books—perhaps in a footnote or two—but he described his bureau as follows:

> *My bureau, though engaged specifically in a work of relief;*
> *though it is the means of feeding the hungry, caring for the*
> *orphans and widows, protecting and promoting education,*
> *and working to secure justice to the weak and oppressed,*
> *nevertheless, partakes of the hatred meted out to all who*

---

[404] Oliver O. Howard, United States military officer, Britannica.

[405] *Autobiography of Oliver Otis Howard, Major-General, United States Army*, Public Addresses Concerning the Freedman (Baker & Taylor Company, 1908).

are caring for the negro. Its friends are sometimes doubtful about its expediency; many think the universal franchise will dispense with it; so that it is not safe to count upon it or its measures as of long continuance. Work then, my friends, while the sun shines. Do what the Government cannot do...[406]

Well now the sun does still shine and this time the federal government and the private sector can work together to do something. The federal government can use its convening authority to bring together federal, state, local, and private sector stakeholders to do what has not been done in a holistic manner to date, and the private sector can assist in the design and implementation of strategies to create market-based outcomes. Elected officials come and go, but as a country and a civil society, this is our chance to achieve something unique, something foundational, and something that can help to change the economic course of this country and secure the intentions of this democracy.

---

[406] *Autobiography of Oliver Otis Howard, Major-General, United States Army* (Baker & Taylor Company, 1908).

President Trump signs the First Step Act into law,
alongside (L to R) is Vice President Pence, Brooke Rollins,
Ja'Ron Smith, Jared Kushner, and Cassidy Luna.

Celebrating the passage of the First Step Act. L to R: Jared Kushner, Jessica Jackson, Brooke Rollins, Van Jones, Ja'Ron Smith, and Cassidy Luna.

White House Staff stand with beneficiaries and advocates of the First Step Act. Back Row (L to R): Erin Haney, Pat Cipollone, Jared Kushner, Ja'Ron Smith, Brooke Rollins, Crystal Munoz, Ivanka Trump, and Pam Bondi. Front Row (L to R): Jessica Jackson, Judith Negron, Tynice Nichole Hall, Kim Kardashian, and Alice Johnson.

Ja'Ron Smith and Chris Pilkerton presenting to Georgetown University's Pivot Program fellows about the impact of the First Step Act and entrepreneurial support for the formerly incarcerated.

President Trump and Vice President Pence meet with staff regarding the executive order on policing. Seated L to R: Ja'Ron Smith, Hope Hicks, Mark Meadows, Jack Rauch, Jared Kushner, Vice President Pence, and Attorney General Barr. On the couch: Chris Pilkerton. Far Back: Cassidy Luna.

Chris Pilkerton meets with U.S. Housing and Urban Development Secretary Ben Carson and Miami Mayor Francis Suarez in advance of an Opportunity Zone Summit in Miami, Florida.

Scott Turner, U.S. Housing and Urban Development Secretary Ben
Carson and Ja'Ron Smith backstage at an Opportunity Zone event.

President Trump, Vice President Pence, Brooke Rollins, and Chris Pilkerton meet with several entrepreneurs in the Roosevelt Room in the White House regarding small business regulatory barriers.

Chris Pilkerton speaks about Opportunity Zones with Mayor Karen Freeman-Wilson of Gary, Indiana, at the National League of Cities Congressional City Conference.

Chris Pilkerton visits with CEO Steve Vairo and COO Todd Brassard of Calumet Electronics in the Upper Peninsula of Michigan. Calumet Electronics participated in President Trump's Pledge to America's Workers.

Ja'Ron Smith reviews the stage before the official launch
of the Platinum Plan, a first-of-its-kind effort to promote
economic empowerment for Black America.

ACKNOWLEDGMENTS

There are many family members, friends, and professors, as well as former and current colleagues, whom the authors would like to thank for their contributions to this book. While it is difficult to account for all of the people that have been critical to their journeys, they would like to acknowledge the contributions of Dr. Leonard Haynes, Jessica Jackson, Jimmy Kemp, Mary McAndrews, Linda McMahon, Brooke Rollins, Steve Smith, Scott Turner, their parents, their siblings, and of course, their much better halves, Ashley and Amanda.

ABOUT THE AUTHORS

Ja'Ron Smith served in several roles at the White House, including deputy assistant to the president for domestic policy, deputy director for the Office of American Innovation, and director of urban affairs and revitalization for the White House Domestic Policy Council. During that time, his work included leading the legislative effort around criminal justice reform and the First Step Act, authoring executive orders and other impactful initiatives on issues related to safe policing and access to capital for minority-owned businesses. He also served as chief policy strategist for enactment of the Opportunity Zones provision in the Tax Cuts and Jobs Act of 2017. Smith was a key negotiator in helping to secure permanent funding for HBCUs under the FUTURE Act. Prior to his post at the White House, he worked for Senator Tim Scott and served on the staff of the House Committee on Financial Services, the Republican Study Committee, the House Republican Conference under then Representative Mike Pence, and the office of Representative J. C. Watts. Smith is the former executive director of the Thurgood Marshall Foundation's Center for Advancing Opportunity. Ja'Ron is currently a partner at Dentons Global Advisors and Senior Fellow for Right on Crime. He holds a BBA from Howard University, and a Master of Divinity from the Howard School of Divinity. He is a proud member of Alpha Phi Alpha.

Chris Pilkerton is a former Cabinet member and head of the U.S. Small Business Administration, serving as both the agency's acting administrator and general counsel. In these roles, he advocated for America's millions of small businesses, advanced manufacturing ecosystems, and associated workforce development initiatives for urban and rural areas. He also served as a White House senior policy advisor and the executive director of the White House Opportunity Now initiative, a government-wide program to support economic empowerment for disadvantaged communities working directly with mayors and governors on local economic initiatives. Pilkerton has worked as chief legal and regulatory strategy officer for the nation's largest nonprofit community development financial institution concentrating on small business support for the underserved, as well as a compliance director at JPMorgan Chase, where he was named one of the "Heroes of the Fortune 500" by *Fortune* magazine for his humanitarian efforts in Liberia. He began his legal career as an assistant district attorney in Manhattan and went on to become senior counsel at the U.S. Securities and Exchange Commission. He has been an executive-in-residence at Johns Hopkins University Carey Business School and Georgetown University McDonough School of Business, the associate director of the Law and Public Policy Program at The Catholic University of America Columbus School of Law (CUA) and a Fulbright Teaching Scholar in Poland. He holds a master's in public administration from Columbia University School of International and Public Affairs, a JD from CUA, a BA from Fairfield University, and a certificate in data analytics from Cornell University College of Business.